MENTAL HEALTH IN THE DEVELOPING WORLD is divided into three main sections. The first describes some of the characteristics of Latin American countries bearing on mental health, such as: an analysis of the social situation; the traditions of the non-Western societies which populate Latin America; urban and rural development; the organization and planning of social programs; mental health; and medical and folk psychiatry. The second section investigates the Pilot Plan of Social Psychiatry (using Colombia as an example), and the third section assesses the relevance of this plan to all of Latin America.

The program described has already had a major impact on government officials, social scientists, and psychiatrists throughout Latin America. In addition to its scientific merits MENTAL HEALTH IN THE DEVELOPING WORLD will become a major reference for those studying how psychological factors influence the political, social, and economic development of a region.

ABOUT THE AUTHORS

MARIO ARGANDOÑA, M.D., is a research Fellow, Cornell Program in Social Psychiatry.
ARI KIEV, M.D., is Clinical Associate Professor of Psychiatry and head of the Cornell Program in Social Psychiatry. He is the author of TRANSCULTURAL PSYCHIATRY and CURANDERISMO: MEXICAN-AMERICAN FOLK PSYCHIATRY, and editor of MAGIC, FAITH, AND HEALING, all published by The Free Press.

D1491254

MENTAL HEALTH
IN THE DEVELOPING WORLD

MENTAL HEALTH IN THE DEVELOPING WORLD ·

A Case Study
in Latin America

Mario Argandoña, M.D.
and
Ari Kiev, M.D.

 THE FREE PRESS, NEW YORK

Collier–Macmillan Limited, London

THE FREE PRESS
A Division of The Macmillan Company
866 Third Avenue, New York, New York 10022

Collier–Macmillan Canada Ltd., Toronto, Ontario

Library of Congress Catalog Card Number: 72–78606

printing number
1   2   3   4   5   6   7   8   9   10

CONTENTS

Preface   ix

PART ONE—PSYCHIATRY IN LATIN AMERICA   1

Chapter 1: Introduction   3
    Latin America: An Overview   3
    The Role of Psychiatry in Latin America   5

Chapter 2: The Latin American Social Situation   6
    Political Traditions   6
    Social Structure   8
    The Psychology of Latin American Classes   9
    The Upper Class   10
    The Middle Classes   11
    The Lower Classes   11
    Problems of Family Life   12

Chapter 3: Non-Western Societies   15
    The Indians   15
    Indian Traditions: An Obstacle to Development 16
    Indian Institutions   17
    Tribal Indians   18
    The African Population   19

Chapter 4: Development in Latin America   21
    The Concept of Development   21
    The Population Explosion   23
    The Rural Crisis   24

Urbanization 25
Unemployment 27
Housing 29
Marginality and Marginalization 30

*Chapter 5: The Organization and Planning of Social
Programs* 33
Social Security 33
Education 34
The University 35
Public Health 36
Social Diseases 38

Chapter 6: Mental Health 41
Psychiatric Services 41
Social Psychiatry 43
Psychiatric Epidemiology 44
✓ Field Surveys 46

Chapter 7: Psychiatry and the Problems of Development 50
The Population Problem 50
Problems of Urbanization and Industrialization 51
Psychiatry and the Lower Classes 52

Chapter 8: Folk Psychiatry 56
Cultural Patterns and Psychiatry 56
The Folk Psychiatry of Hispanic American Indians 57
The Folk Psychiatry of Tribal Indians 61
The Folk Psychiatry of Afro Americans 63

PART TWO—PILOT PLAN OF SOCIAL PSYCHIATRY (PPSP) 69

Chapter 9: The Nation and the City 71
Colombia 71
Geography 71
History 72
Population and Development 73
"La Violencia" 74
Health Resources 74
Mental Health 76
Cali 77

The Department of Psychiatry of the Facultad de Medecina
de Universidad del Valle   79

Chapter 10: PPSP Rationale and Locale   83
    Clarification of Objectives   83
    Description of Facilities   86
    El Guabal   87
    San Juan Bautista, The Parochial Center   89
    Candelaria   91

Chapter 11: Educational Activities   94
    The Place of Education in Mental Health   94
    Training Psychiatrists   95
    Training Medical Students and Physicians   100
    Training Allied Personnel   102
    Educating the Public   109

Chapter 12: Organizational Activities   113
    Organization of Functions   113
    Integration of Teamwork   114
    Teamwork Functions   115
    Leadership Functions   118

Chapter 13: Research   122
    The Need for Research   122
    The Epidemiological Approach   124
    Epidemiological Research in PPSP   125
    Data from Registered Patients   126
    Field Surveys   133

PART THREE—THE PPSP AND LATIN AMERICA   141

Chapter 14: Assessment   143
    Antecedents   143
    Field Work   144

Chapter 15: Practicability   148
    Latin America's Crisis   148
    Psychiatric Help   149
    The Example of PPSP   150

Chapter 16: Optional Models 154
   The PPSP as a National Plan 154
   Local Action 155
   Alternative Approaches 156
   Prerequisites 158

Chapter 17: Looking at the Future 161
   The Need for Expansion 161
   Education 162
   Research 164
   Therapy and Prevention of Illness 165
   Organization 166

Epilogue 169

Index 171

PREFACE

MEDICAL programs in developing countries generally have a much lower priority than those for industrialization, rural development and food production and for medical programs: Psychiatric programs usually have the lowest. Widespread malnutrition, high infant and child mortality rates, and shortened life expectancies because of infectious diseases are given much more attention.

The great cost to society of untreated psychiatric disorders is obviously underestimated. Unlike other illnesses, the extent of which can readily be calculated from morbidity and mortality statistics, psychiatric illnesses, particularly the less severe disorders, do not lend themselves so readily to enumeration. Often they manifest themselves in ways which are not readily recognized. Much of the absenteeism which so seriously affects the manpower pools of the developing nations is often due to psychiatric illness. Similarly, high rates of social disorders such as narcotic addiction, alcoholism, prostitution, and child exploitation are in large measure related to the presence of psychiatric disorders. Of even greater importance is their presence in persons in crucial positions of leadership who may cause irreparable harm to the development of their societies.

If development and human resources are to be encouraged, psychiatric programs must receive more attention. Psychiatric illness must be recognized in terms of such effects on the social system as unemployability, absenteeism, lack of motivation, delinquency, crime, drug addiction, and alcoholism, as well as susceptibility to revolution, violence, and social turmoil.

Psychiatric disorders are chronic conditions which reduce the work force, swell the welfare rolls, and produce social and economic burdens far greater than is suggested by the hospital admission data on severe disorders only. Psychiatric disorders may also have serious consequences for the mental, physical, and social well-being of other family members, in particular the children. This ultimately may be reflected in social performance.

The high cost of caring for patients in poorly staffed, custodial institutions filled with chronic, long-term patients is also insufficiently considered when determining priorities. Maintaining these large institutions often costs more than community treatment.

Furthermore, the traditional one-to-one psychiatric-patient model of modern psychiatry is not applicable to the developing societies, where there are insufficient psychiatrists for the number of patients. The rationale that the "successful analysis" of a single individual can significantly affect many others does not justify the intensive time investment required by dynamic psychotherapeutic treatment. Developing countries must recognize that the public health model already being used is relevant for psychiatric problems and can be adapted to incorporate a psychiatric approach. Paramedical personnel, technical specialists, and large-scale treatment programs to the developing world.

A Model for Developing Countries
with Considerable Resources

In Latin America, facilities, personnel, and training programs for ancillary personnel are available to a much greater extent than in other developing areas; they provide an infrastructure onto which new programs can be grafted. Colombia, for example, has 140 psychiatrists; 16 in Cali, 90 in Bogotá, 19 in Medellin, and 15 scattered around in other cities. While these psychiatrists serve 18 million people and are, moreover, in the urban centers, they nevertheless represent a considerable advance beyond the least developed societies and afford a foundation for developing new programs. There are also a number of psychiatric hospitals in these cities, from which expanded efforts could begin. In Bogotá, there are 8 psychiatric hospitals, 1 state hospital, and 1 facility at the university level. In Cali, there is a university psychiatric hospital with 250 beds, along with two other mental-health clinics, which have 40 beds. In Medellin, there are 1,454 beds, 4 hospitals, and 1 university hospital.

A primary objective is to maximize the existing facilities and personnel so as to bring more people into the treatment network, at earlier periods in their illness, and to coordinate social welfare and follow-up programs so as to reduce the need for subsequent hospitalization. Strategy should include:

1. A case register of all patients and programs for systematic follow-ups, utilizing public health nurses, midwives, welfare workers, and others who are already in touch with these patients in their communities.

2. A program of comprehensive family medical care whereby a case worker will be assigned to entire families in a given community to facilitate early case identification, reduce the fragmentation of services and agencies, and diminish the frequently encountered resistance to psychiatric care among the poor.

3. A national health scheme for assigning people to particular clinics by districts so as to ensure comprehensive coverage of the entire population, whether or not they are under treatment.

4. Expansion of the traidtional role of the psychiatrist and other professionals in the education and training of others. New programs should start at the level of existing needs. Paramedical personnel must be trained to replace physicians wherever possible, thereby allowing physicians more time to supervise and develop new programs. Health teams make it possible to delegate treatment responsibilities to people of different skills at different phases in treatment. This approach amplifies the effectiveness of the physician and at the same time increases the number of patients who can be seen. The "team model" for delivering care is especially applicable to drug-oriented community psychiatric programs; it is feasible in countries where a range of experts exists.

The health team should include physicians, psychiatrists, sanitary engineers, population control experts, and behavioral scientists—all of whom can contribute to mental health programs, not only in traditional ways but through the control of sanitation, the improvement of nutrition, and the management of population movements, all of which have significant pathogenic effects in the developing countries.

The major task in a country as advanced as Colombia is thus not the development of a primary facility, or the training of a basic core team, but the allocation of resources in the most useful fashion. The opportunity exists in such countries to develop new models for delivering care, in line with geographic and residential patterns. The major cities have low-income barrios, with medical clinics that maintain nutritional, birth control, anti-tuberculosis, and sanitation programs. Contact with the population of the barrio makes it a particularly useful place to introduce mental health programs. At this level, patients can be seen early in their illness, thereby preventing the need for hospitalization. The clinics are particularly useful for training residents and medical students, who are assigned to them on a rotating basis. Universities can establish contact with them and thus form the vanguard in community mental health programs. Leading citizens, as well as general practitioners and specialists in internal medicine, can form community mental health boards to help implement the programs. The barrio clinic offers the psychiatrist direct access to the population, in that way enabling him to initiate a variety of anthropological, sociological, and transcultural psychiatric studies. Methodologically adequate epidemiological studies can be carried out because of the existence of comprehensive information on the population.

In 1967, such a program was developed through the Universidad del Valle in Cali, Colombia. Utilizing local medical personnel, it was established in three public health centers, in two barrios, Guabal and Villa Nueva, and in the rural area of Candelaria. The objective was to treat in the community and thus avoid unnecessary hospitalization. The main task of the resident psychiatrist was to spend one day a week in each clinic, training the non-psychiatric physicians and senior medical students in psychiatric diagnosis and treatment, as well as running meetings for various community groups and engaging the participation of community leaders. During the first year at the clinic in Guabal, 75 patients were seen, 205 consultations were carried out, 19 classes were held, 10 public lectures for patients were held, and 20 doctors and 10 school teachers were trained in the rudiments of psychiatric diagnosis and treatment. From its inception in August 1967 to June 1969, the clinic in Guabal (population 17,500) provided extra-mural care to 184 adults and 143 children.

This sort of program is feasible in countries, like Colombia, where long-term follow-up of psychiatric patients can be carried out by public health nurses and non-psychiatric personnel in remote provincial clinics. The maintenance of drug therapy for specified periods, and the early identification of recurrent episodes, are essential to its success. In addition, periodic examinations have the added features of reducing unnecessary referrals to over-crowded central facilities and facilitating the combined medical and psychiatric management of patients who are suffering from both physical and emotional illnesses. With such a scheme, it is possible to identify problem families, with various physical and mental disorders, who can be treated by a team, thus avoiding the fragmentation of services and preventing the accumulation of large groups of custodial cases.

The program described in this book was developed by Ari Kiev and Carlos Leon, M.D., Professor of Psychiatry, Universidad del Valle, Cali, Colombia, with the support of the International Committee Against Mental Illness and its President, Nathan S. Kline, M.D. Mario Argandona worked in the program during its first year of operation, and as a research fellow in the Cornell Program in Social Psychiatry, during which time this book was written.

This book describes the application of certain psychiatric techniques in an urbanizing Latin American community.

The first part of this book describes some of the characteristics of Latin American countries bearing on mental health.

The second part deals with a pilot plan of social psychiatry in a South American city.

The third part discusses the applicability of the pilot plan to other Latin American areas.

PART ONE

Psychiatry in Latin America

CHAPTER 1

Introduction

LATIN AMERICA: AN OVERVIEW

LATIN AMERICA is facing a crisis; political instability and economic weakness hinder any plan to eradicate hunger, poverty, and social misery. Massive migration to the cities and the population explosion compound frustration arising from inability to adjust to the requirements of changing situations. People trusting tradition (God or paternalistic institutions) fail to give up their conservative attitudes for economic progress.

Bitter resentment or fatalistic apathy account for the existing tension and despair that pervade Latin American society and further slow development and progress, although Latin Americans also share mutual hopes, needs, interests, and goals.

At present, the group of nations located south of the Rio Grande has the greatest development potential of the underdeveloped three-quarters of the world. In distribution of land and population, Latin America has one-seventh of the earth's land surface; but only one-fourteenth of the world population lives in the region, and it is concentrated mostly in coastal zones or unproductive areas which are favorable for trade but not for agriculture. More than half of the subcontinent is uncultivated, fertile land.

Latin America's economic development is, however, becoming less and less a function of its agriculture. Extractive industries predominate in a number of countries. These activities are basically concentrated in accessible coastal zones, despite the fact that mineral wealth, especially oil, is concentrated in inland areas.

Prospects for industry are based on the capacity for generating energy which could be obtained from the enormous rivers that come down from the Andes and cross Latin American soil. Rivers are also potential communication channels.

Although obsolete traditions are still significant, Western culture predominates and, considering the population, Huenlin points out that:

> It would be misleading to suggest that all the population and governments of Latin America are inert, poverty-ridden and incapable of creative effort. Experience in small scale in several countries, especially those with some indigenous and mestizo population, suggest that backward communities in remote districts are capable of remarkable feats of self-help once they are given professional guidance and the basic tools with which to work. The major obstacles have hitherto been ignorance and hopelessness, both basically the consequence of official neglect. . . . The deduction to be made from experiences of this kind is that social services and local communications can be improved in countless areas with a minimum of expenditure.[1]

Latin America is held back by its disparities. It contains one country that is too large to be governed effectively, Brazil, with a population of 85 million occupying a vast, rich territory of more than 8.5 sq. km. In contrast, there are several countries too small to be economically viable. El Salvador, for example, is 130 times smaller than Argentina, and Mexico has 37 times the population of Panama. In some areas—El Salvador with a density of 139 population per sq. km., and Haiti with 166—the pressure of rapidly growing population on inadequate land is resulting in malnutrition. In other areas there is not enough population to make land productive: in Bolivia population density is only 3 inhabitants per sq. km.

Social and cultural structures differ in different countries. In

Argentina and Uruguay, where the population is almost entirely of European origin, the culture is quite homogeneous. In countries like Brazil, Colombia, and Venezuela, the complex ethnic structure has not been an obstacle to the spread of Western culture. But in Central America and the Andean Highlands, a large Indian population preserves pre-Columbian ways of life. Haiti is an exception, as its homogeneous population and culture are not widely open to significant influences from Western culture.

THE ROLE OF PSYCHIATRY IN LATIN AMERICA

The disparities and paradoxes just mentioned are of secondary importance. It is necessary to know not only the special features of each country, but also their similarities.

The value of psychiatry to the process of development has not been recognized. Psychiatry can assist governments in understanding the effects of social turmoil on the individual, his family, and his community.

NOTES

1. Wall, W. D., *Education and Mental Health*, Paris, UNESCO, 1955, pp. 14–18.
2. Eisemberg, Leon, "Preventive Psychiatry, If Not Now, When?" *International Trends in Mental Health*, Henry P. David (Ed.), New York, McGraw-Hill, 1966, p. 63.
3. Rees, J. R., "The World Community," p. 5.
4. Murphy, H. B. M., "Social Changes and Mental Health," in *Causes of Mental Disorders: A Review of Epidemiological Knowledge*, New York, Milbank Memorial Fund, 1961, p. 280.
5. Huenlin, D., "Latin America: A Summary of Economic Problems," in *Latin America and the Caribbean, A Handbook*, Claudio Veliz (Ed.), New York, Praeger, 1968, p. 472.

CHAPTER 2

The Latin American
Social Situation

POLITICAL TRADITIONS

IN spite of the optimism that has been nurtured in the United States
and the Latin American countries themselves about the growth of
democracy, no improvement has occurred. The fate of the Alliance
for Progress illustrates this failure. In the seven years since its
launching, which made financial aid from the United States con-
ditional on the implementation of democratic practices, there have
been 14 military coups in 9 countries.

According to Veliz, the explanation for these failures lies in
Latin American political traditions.[1]

A strong centralist tradition, along with colonial bureaucracy
and its hierarchical tendencies, was transferred to Latin America
from Spain during the early days of Spanish colonization. The re-
bellions of 1810, instead of beginning a liberal tradition, marked
instead a massive transfer of central power from Madrid to each

republic's capital. This collective experience (with the exception of Brazil) largely accounts for the role which authoritarian centralism has played in Latin American history. Latin America stands now on the frontier of ideology; none of those political, economic, or social systems based on the European experience during the Industrial Revolution seems to apply. Yet the growing population and new forms of social organization and economic aspirations demand action. So far, the traditional, urban, non-industrial, middle class (which includes the military) has been unable to create viable social and political arrangements. At the same time, the hope that the peasantry or the lower strata of the urban population will play the role which the industrial bourgeoisie played in Europe seems illusory. Thus, Latin America has gradually returned to her traditions of centralism, bearing a strong imprint of paternalism and a vast bureaucratic mechanism with a formidable respect for legality and authority.

In religion, just as in political affairs, there have been no peripheral sites of power—the Catholic Church has not lost its privileged, unchallenged, doctrinal position.

One of the consequences of centralization of power and uniform acceptance of political and religious authority was the absence of an industrial revolution in the European sense. In Latin America the rise of industry has not brought about substantial changes in the distribution of power—far from it: industrialization has depended directly on state intervention, and success for the entrepreneur is more dependent on good relations with the central government than on technical or commercial efficiency. Also, the state handles foreign exchange in ways which recall the patronage of the Spanish imperial tradition.

Under paternalistic centralism, the semi-literate Latin American population cherished a "dependency wish," a desire to earn personal protection through loyalty. The implicit political potential was used by the caudillos (popular leaders), who, because of their ability to express the wishes and feelings of the masses, ultimately gained power. The power of the caudillos was determined by a generally accepted notion of the "patron state"—which the caudillos had fashioned for themselves.

Another consequence of centralism fostered by the pressure of popular groups (populism) is the charismatic nature of the *caudillos* (popular leaders). As the old ties of dependence on legitimate traditional authority gradually disappeared, the *caudillos* identified the lower social classes with state institutions. The leaders and ideologists of populism reverted to the old principle which sees in the people the sole source of authority and power.[2]

Toward the end of the nineteenth century, the incompetence of the *caudillo* in battle gave an impetus to reform and more professionalism in the military. A decline in the number of military coups in the early twentieth century encouraged the view that professionalism would weaken the tendency of soldiers to intervene in politics. However, since 1930 there have been over 100 violent changes of power in Latin America (during this period only Mexico has suffered no military coup) nor is there any sign today that military intervention is diminishing.[3] The military follows the trend toward absolute central power.

SOCIAL STRUCTURE

The concentration of political and religious power fostered a rigid paternalism—the "patronage" system—based on the perpetuation of a two-class society of powerful rulers and servile followers. Thus, opportunities open to various social groups were highly unequal. Paternalism accounts for the fact that values like competition, merit, and technical efficiency, as principles of social organization, cannot play the same role in Latin America as in more advanced industrial societies. Such a system may be progressive when the *patrones* are endowed with a modern consciousness, but becomes regressive the moment the *patrones* see a threat to their security or their social prestige.

In such a society, social mobility is almost impossible and the upper classes develop a parasitic way of life, availing themselves of the relative advantages they have secured rather than striving for a new social organization. However,

During the period since 1961, the Latin American governments have entered into a series of commitments to accelerate development and promote social justice within a framework of long-term planning and regional integration.[4]

Although Latin America has progressed both materially and in its ability to coordinate regional action, actual development, involving far-reaching shifts in the roles and power relationships of different groups in society, is bound to be advanced by some groups and resisted by others. Some question the validity of the two-class society and advocate a society with many social strata. This involves considerable movement from one stratum to another and an expectation of continuing socio-economic change.

In Latin America:

> . . . the picture of growing middle classes as sources of dynamism and political stability is replaced by the picture of the existing middle classes of the region as beneficiaries and defenders of existing structural rigidities, barriers to the effective incorporation of the marginal strata into national societies.[5]

THE PSYCHOLOGY OF LATIN AMERICAN CLASSES

Pervasive tension and a feeling of urgency combine with dissatisfaction with the present and an uneasiness concerning the future. Accusations are made that reforms are being blocked by vested interests. Many Latin American elites, unwilling to accept a social order that permits popular participation, support military regimes that would protect the traditional order.[6] Overt dependence on populistic-traditionalistic leaders and suspicion of new patterns of social organization reinforce the maintenance of traditional attitudes to the detriment of social development and psychological adjustment. This is well illustrated in the case of industrialization problems which develop in various ways:

1. The traditional structures are dislocated without being replaced by new structures, affecting the family, the local community, the position of young people, and political conflicts.
2. Conflicts arise between various sectors of society, facing the individual with opposing requirements and no solution. These

conflicts may spring from the coexistence of attitudes, norms, and values which belong to different stages of social development.

3. The change takes place so rapidly that adaptation cannot occur. This relates to the problem of mass rural migration. The individual finds himself deprived of social frames of reference to guide his behavior and thoughts.[7]

THE UPPER CLASSES

Lipset's recent survey of Latin American elites provides useful distinctions for analyzing the relation between values and the conditions for development: achievement-ascription, universalism-particularism, specificity-diffuseness and egalitarianism-elitism.[8]

A society's value system may emphasize treating others in terms of their abilities and performances (achievement) or in terms of inherited qualities (ascription), applying to them a general standard (universalism) or responding to some personal attribute or relationship (particularism), and dealing with them in terms of their specific positions (specificity) or in general terms as members of the collective (diffuseness). An egalitarian society does not imply lack of differences in power, income, wealth, or status, but it does tend to place more emphasis on universalistic criteria in interpersonal judgment, and less on elitist hierarchical differences.

Although no society is totally egalitarian, ascriptive, or universalistic, Latin American upper classes are basically ascriptive, particularistic, diffuse, and elitist, meaning that in such groups, authority and power tend to be focused around kinship and the local community. Such a system will naturally oppose centralized authority and will see work achievement as a necessary evil. Morality will be equated with the acceptance of the *status quo* and the acceptance of progress—insofar as it means social upheaval—will evoke ambivalent attitudes. These assumptions have been confirmed by the observation of foreign-born entrepreneurs who reach a social scale based on their "deviant" orientations: once they reach the upper stratum, they shift from their original values to those of the surrounding aristocracy and raise their children conventionally.

THE MIDDLE CLASSES

Throughout Latin America social relationships have been dependent on sponsorship (whether by relatives, friends, or a political party) rather than an open competition for advancement. This background, combined with the importance of public employment opportunities for middle-class youth, has contributed to a reliance on government action for the solution of all problems that inhibit the innovating spirit of a rising middle class.[9]

The middle classes are undergoing various stresses that will affect their futures. In most countries, the lower-middle groups are barely able to afford consumer goods that they have come to think of as essential to a "decent" way of life; and the widening demand for TV sets and other consumer products indicates that this strain on their incomes will be even greater in the future. Debt is widespread and thrift is dying as inflation rises. Satisfaction with present levels of living is therefore low. It is significant that while groups falling within the narrower definitions of the middle classes, such as teachers or bank employees, have been among the most frequent and militant participants in strikes in recent years, the psychological attitude of the middle class sectors generally has tended toward enjoyment of the privileges they have acquired. The population has lapsed into a generalized resignation in politics and in economics in the face of the frustrations of everyday life.[10]

THE LOWER CLASSES

The lower classes' difficulties derive in part from the need to turn agricultural manpower into a disciplined labor force.

Perhaps the most important reason for rural migration to urban areas is the belief that greater opportunities exist in cities. Whether the expectations of those moving to cities are fulfilled is less important than their conviction. But the difficulties encountered by migrant workers and their families at first may even be greater than the ones they left behind.

The migrant is moving from a system based on barter and

property to more complex systems based on money and contract, which are inherently more complex. The almost impossible task of grasping the new concepts and discipline demanded by money and technology further increases the insecurity of the uprooted newcomer.

According to one report from the United Nations:

> We have little evidence about the ways in which urban lower classes are adjusting to urban society. Observers in some localities report a pathetic misery and little or no upward mobility but other local groups are reported to be striving desperately to better their lot through education, acquisition of skills and self-help organizations.
>
> Among many of them, occupational preferences, family life, and residence seem to be equally unstable; the men may try to relieve their burden by shifting from job to job, by deserting their families or by moving to another town. They are less likely to be active members of formal organizations of any kind than are the groups above them in the social scale. Many of them are frequent cinema-goers and have radios in their homes; in the larger cities, a few of them have even managed to acquire television sets. Newspapers and other periodicals appealing to the semi-literate have grown in numbers and in circulation. We know very little, however, of the nature of the influence exerted by these media on the masses of the urban (let alone the rural) population. . . . Observers point to a continuing rejection of impersonal urban institutions and work relationships, a yearning for person-to-person guidance and aid, replacing that once expected from the *patrones,* the paternalistic landowner. It is well known that a few leaders in different countries offering personal magnetism, sympathy and simple solutions to their problems have had remarkable success in drawing large previously alienated sectors of the population into active participation in national life, while at the same time fostering among them expectations and hostilities that can hardly be reconciled with present developmental needs.[11]

PROBLEMS OF FAMILY LIFE

Much more research is required about the effect of urbanization and social change on family life in Latin America. One can only assume that a well-adjusted family life is difficult to maintain during a period of transition.

According to reports from the United Nations:

It is known that there are large numbers of irregular families in the slums of most of the [Latin American] larger cities, families in which the lack of a permanent male partner who assumes responsibility for support of the children condemns the latter to extreme poverty and undernourishment, and drives many boys [and girls] into the street at an early age to forage for a living through odd jobs and petty theft. . . .

There appears to be no general and consistent pattern of strong rural families versus disorganized urban families, but a wide variety of forms of family organization and disorganization are trends therein both in the cities and in the countryside.[12]

Some sources of insecurity and disorganization, hard to assess, lie in an increased freedom for women, which, because of its unexpected and rapid appearance, has not yet led to generally accepted new codes of behavior and family life.[13] Women are becoming better educated, better informed, and less inclined to be subservient. Now they have the right to vote and they exercise that right.[14]

For many of the migrants, the conjugal or nuclear family may replace a rural extended family. The extended family is more characteristic, however, of the (mainly urban) upper class than of the peasants and rural workers. The peasants' extended family ties usually do not include joint households or joint cultivation of land. Family obligations are purposely broadened by the *compadrazgo* (godparenthood) system.

The maintenance of primary ties of kinship offer a strategy to ensure individual survival in the major towns. The perpetuation of certain traditional family patterns helps especially to mitigate urban unemployment:

The social norms prescribing mutual aid among kinfolk—and the stretched circle of solidarity which goes beyond kinfolk proper— may have enabled some members of the group to depend wholly or partly on those who were receiving regular remuneration or income. . . .

In many families the survival of the group depends upon individual contributions to the communal economy of the family, which sometimes meant that two or more families shared the same housing unit for periods of varying length.[15]

The solidarity of the family group may also permit upward social mobility and the conservation of individual status.

So far, we have described the adjustment of traditional family patterns to living conditions in the cities of Latin America; now, we will see how these patterns influence urban institutional structures. "Familism" and its influence on politics, the structure of administration, business, and enterprise are typical of the cities in each of the Latin American republics. Thus, familism as a model for the organization of human relations seems to have taken deep root in most of the new and supposedly impersonal institutional systems. Sometimes familistic relations were of help in integrating these institutions; at other times it seemed family structures might have been a factor militating against the full development of these organizations.[16]

NOTES

1. Veliz, Claudio (Ed.), "An Historical Introduction," in *Latin America and the Caribbean, A Handbook.*

2. U.N., *Social Development of Latin America in the Post-War Period*, E/CN. 12/660, 1964.

3. Hennesy, A., "The Military in Politics," in *Latin America and the Caribbean, A Handbook,* Claudio Veliz (Ed.), p. 366.

4. U.N., *1967 Report on the World Social Situation*, p. 125.

5. *Ibid.*, p. 130.

6. *Ibid.* Although "the military are now turning towards progressive attitudes," see *The Rockefeller Report on the Americas,* Chicago, Quadrangle Books, 1969, pp. viii and 32.

7. Hauser, P. M., *Urbanization in Latin America*, UNESCO, 1967, pp. 53–4.

8. Lipset, S. M., "Values, Education and Entrepreneurship," in *Elites in Latin America,* S. M. Lipset and A. Solari (Eds.), New York, Oxford University Press, 1967.

9. U.N., *1963 World Social Situation*, p. 126.

10. U.N., *Social Development of Latin America in the Post-War Period,* p. 111.

11. U.N., *1963 Report on the World Social Situation*, p. 127.

12. U.N., *1957 Report on the World Social Situation*, p. 190.

13. U.N., *1963 Report on the World Social Situation*, p. 126.

14. *The Rockefeller Report*, p. 136.

15. U.N., *Social Development of Latin America in the Post-War Period,* p. 68.

16. *Ibid.*, pp. 67–9.

CHAPTER 3

Non-Western Societies

THE INDIANS

THE term *indio* (or *indigena*) may be used to refer to physical features of the pre-Hispanic inhabitants of America, but it is more frequently used as a social and cultural term, rather than a racial one.

As Adams says:

An indian is an individual who is recognized and who recognizes himself as belonging to a community of individuals that are in turn called Indians. Such communities are characterized by certain formal cultural features which set them aside from the rest of the national population.[1]

The Indian population of Latin America is today a poor sector of peasants and laborers.

Indians are prominent in Mexico, through Central America to

the Andean highlands, and especially in Ecuador, Peru, and Bolivia.

All these countries suffer an "Indian problem." Lack of development is in part due to a mass of Indians who are resistant, culturally and personally, to civilization and progress; the problem is why, after 400 years of functional interdependence in economic and social life, the Indian peasantry should still be culturally separated from the rest of the society and subject to it. Pearse notes that ". . . the question is one of problem societies and not of problem races or problem cultures."[2]

INDIAN TRADITIONS: AN OBSTACLE TO DEVELOPMENT

Although the Indian has shown little impetus to change during the last three decades, he has been moving toward class consciousness and aspiring to values hitherto considered out of his reach. This trend is demonstrated in the watchword of the Mexican Indian Institute, "To redeem the Indian is to redeem the nation." In Bolivia, the Indians have shown the most promising signs of entering into their political heritage.[3] Development, however, carries a threat to four centuries of a static way of life adapted to the social and physical environment.

The effects of rapid changes on the inheritors of Indian and Spanish traditions have been studied most carefully in the cultural enclave of nearly 4 million Spanish Americans and Mexican Americans living side by side with members of the dominant American culture in five Southwestern states. These people are, historically and geographically, from the fringe of Latin American culture, language, and religion. Spanish and Mexican Americans are under the most intense pressure to renounce obsolete traditions and to become oriented to modern values. Opportunities for change increase from day to day, but Indian–Spanish culture remains clearly defined in spite of the Anglo–American impact. A UNESCO publication states:

In the face of differing dominant culture, of rapid technological change around them, they maintained the values, the concepts, the attitudes of their fathers, not through ignorance of another way of life, but by choice. They accepted a few traits from the "Anglo" culture, plucked them out of context and gave them ther own background. They took electricity for their houses, but in general they reject running water and plumbing, because these were manipulations of nature, with which they were familiar and intimate. They play basketball, and light a candle to the saint for aid in winning. They accepted schooling, but not the"Anglo" motivations for education—the higher standard of living, the better job. . . . When they become urbanized, they reproduce their village community and buy a piece of land to till. They choose and reject according to their system of values.[4]

As in the rest of Latin America, these people are in daily contact with the dominant group, at work, at school, and in politics.

Hispanic American Indians have been deprived of much of their land. They are now suspicious of innovations and afraid of schemes for land improvement and legal documents. On the other hand, they are in daily contact with technology and Western habits, adopting many of them gradually.

INDIAN INSTITUTIONS

The market places in Guatemalan or Bolivian villages, the Inca ruins at Machu-Pichu, and the famous temple-pyramids which are vestiges of the Maya civilization in Mexico are only a few examples of the importance of the Indian heritage. The Maya calendar still regulates the farming process of Guatemalan Indians, and the Indian's world is still shaped by myth and magic.[5]

Sometimes a remarkable degree of cultural synthesis has occurred, as in Paraguay, where Guarani ranks with Spanish as the medium for conversation or literature. Other times, as in Peru, two disparate worlds coexist in symbiosis. The Indian institutions continue to demonstrate everywhere their tenacious capacity for survival, if not for "progress."

The more obvious aspects of Indian life concern domestic areas: clothing, methods of cooking and farming, and home industries such as pottery, basketware, and textile products are prominent.

Indian influence is also present in regional dances and music. Perhaps more important are those vestiges which persist where not a word of Indian language is now spoken; shamans and *curanderos,* for example, can be found in the Southwest United States.[6] Indians are devout Christians, but they have developed unique religious practices such as the sponsorship of feasts in honor of their favorite patron saint, the visitation of burial grounds on All Saints' and All Souls' Days, and complex beliefs about the presence of spirits— *animas*—and their return to earth to visit relatives. Songs, folk dances, etc., express this animism.

Another institution is the *compadrazgo,* or co-parenthood, which is a method of extending mutual obligations between parents and godparents to as many people as possible.

Perhaps the most striking of all Indian institutions is cooperative work. Its private form is the preparation of *chicha* (corn beer) by a group of men and women who chew the flower before the brewing. Families help each other in the construction of their dwellings. In its public form this cooperation is extended to communal tasks like building a school and repairing roads or channels.[7]

We may assume that this consciousness of very closely knit groups would make adaptation to the individualistic system of relationships in modern urban life difficult.

TRIBAL INDIANS

Besides the descendants of highly organized pre-Columbian civilizations, there are Indians who belong to small tribes, mainly in the tropical forests of South America.

These tribes persist today at a primitive level. A U.N. report notes:

> Reports of anthropologists and accounts of atrocities that occasionally reach the press, indicate that the advance of roads and land settlement is even now accompanied by seizure of tribal lands, elimination of previous sources of livelihood such as hunting, introduction of new diseases and even massacres of groups consid-

ered dangerous by the settlers. Whole tribes continue to be extinguished.[8]

This situation contrasts with that attained by the Andean Indian. Unfortunately, the national governments are unable to protect the Indian tribes of remote lowlands which are not yet integrated into the social and economic life of the nation.

In spite of their importance for anthropological psychiatry, these tribes are the least known human groups on earth.

THE AFRICAN POPULATION

The slave trade, which lasted well into the nineteenth century, distributed African people and culture throughout the Caribbean area—the islands and the continental shores of Spanish colonies—and coastal Brazil. These people worked primarily on sugar cane plantations. Since colonial days, Afro–Americans have influenced the lower urban and rural classes in these areas and their culture plays an important role in the system of social relationships and beliefs within the "culture of poverty." One of its particular traits is the singular position of women. Ribeiro[9] has described the economic, social, and sexual freedom allowed women, which led to common-law marriages, transitional male partners, and mother-centered households.

After centuries of interaction with Roman Catholicism and European culture, there are Afro–American cults which are heavily overlaid with Christian syncretism, with a good deal of local variety (see Chapter 9). It is interesting that while such cult groups exist in Cuba, Jamaica, Haiti, Trinidad, the Guyanas, and coastal Brazil, they are absent in the Dominican Republic, Puerto Rico, Colombia, Venezuela, and Central America.[10] It seems likely that the establishment of the Inquisition in Mexico and Cartagena-de-Indias during the early period of Spanish dominance prevented the development of non-Catholic rites in these neighboring colonies. Wherever these cults exist, their distinguishing factor is a spiritualism involving possession-trance seances with largely therapeutic goals.

NOTES

1. Adams, R. N., "The Indians of Central America," in *Latin America and the Caribbean, A Handbook,* Claudio Veliz (Ed.), p. 696.
2. Pearse, A., "The Indians of the Andes," *ibid.,* p. 691.
3. Clissold, S., "The Indian Heritage," *ibid.,* pp. 756–7.
4. Mead, Margaret (Ed.), *Cultural Patterns and Technical Change,* UNESCO, Mentor Books, 1955, p. 151.
5. Coy, P., "The Indians of Mexico," in *Latin America and the Caribbean, A Handbook,* Claudio Veliz (Ed.), p. 706.
6. Kiev, Ari, *Curanderismo, Mexican-American Folk Psychiatry,* New York, The Free Press, 1968.
7. Coy, *loc. cit.*
8. U.N., *1967 Report on the World Social Situation,* p. 137.
9. Ribeiro, R., *Male Homosexuality and Afro-Brazilian Religion,* Universidad Federal de Pernambuco, 1968 (typescript).
10. Bourgignon, E., "World Distribution and Patterns of Possession States," in *Trance and Possession States,* Raymond Prince (Ed.), Montreal, R. M. Bucke, Mem. Soc., 1968.

CHAPTER 4

Development
in Latin America

THE CONCEPT OF
DEVELOPMENT

ACCORDING to an American scholar, "development" is a term generally used to describe the kind of economic and social changes that are occurring in the so-called "Third World" after the impact of the expansion of technology and industry of Western culture. Conversely, it is said that development is a kind of change that affects a given society aiming to equate ". . . the social structures, technology and life styles that exist today in the Western countries of Europe, the United States and the Soviet Union," that is to say, the so-called "First and Second World."[1] However, very few inhabitants of the "Third World" would accept these concepts; we have already seen how Latin American societies either reject or distrust numerous Western institutions. Development, therefore, must achieve better standards of living and social justice without necessarily supplanting useful traditions.

Lipset illustrates this necssity:

> The experience of Japan, the one non-Western nation which has successfully industrialized, suggests that the key question may not be creation of new values so much as the way in which cultural ideals supporting tradition can give rise to those supporting modernity, that the shift from tradition to modernity need not involve a total rejection of a nation's basic values.[2]

The fact is that the conception of development depends both on the faith in, and on the consciousness of, change.

The definition of development in terms of per capita output and rates of capital investment has become standard currency for all economists. Another approach emphasizes the products of advanced technology, but to equate development with rapid and high industrialism is to avoid a number of critical issues.

A report from the United Nations points out that in Latin America:

> Some studies are going beyond these interpretations to a more fundamental and controversial criticism of the kinds of economic growth and social change that are taking place. It is argued that such growth, even if it manages to attain for a time satisfactory rates in *per capita* income, is inherently bound up with widening inequalities between the region as a whole and the regions previously industrialized; between the great cities, the smaller urban centers and the countryside; and between social strata within the countries.[3]

Latin American countries are indeed at widely different levels of economic growth and social integration; therefore, the term "underdeveloped" is now less appropriate than "unevenly developed"; nevertheless, the process of change and development is conspicuous everywhere and apparently accelerating.

In the quest for development, several broad problem areas have arisen as facets of a single problem. These are: the population explosion, rural crises associated with stagnation of production and partial disintegration of former systems, rapid and concentrated urbanization, lack of productive employment for a labor force with high rates of growth and low levels of qualification, and the emergence and rapid growth of new kinds of marginal population strata unassimilated in national structures of production, consumption, and political participation.

The dimensions of these problems, during the last decades, have been affected very little by development policies and plans.

THE POPULATION EXPLOSION

From about 250 million at present, the population of Latin America should reach 300 million before 1975 and 600 million by the year 2000.[4] With an approximate average annual growth rate of 3.1 per cent in 1968, the 20 countries of Latin America are the fastest growing in the world.[5] The enormous reduction in mortality in Latin America has not been matched by an increase in the standard of living for the majority.

A second variable controlling population growth, fertility, having social, cultural, and ethical determinants, has remained very much at its pre-modern, rather high level.

The unusual combination of declining mortality with high and stabilized fertility, besides accelerating growth, produces a large proportion of children and young adults. The proportion of persons under 14 years of age averages about 40 per cent of the total population (ranging from 28 per cent in Uruguay to 48.8 per cent in Guatemala). On the other hand, the proportion of persons over 60 years of age is very small: between 4 to 6 per cent for the whole region, from 2.5 per cent in Honduras, to 8.9 per cent in Argentina.[6]

In spite of the fact that the extremely youthful population means high ratios of dependants and heavy burdens on public facilities, most of the Latin American countries resist the idea of rapid population growth as the key problem of Latin America.

In the short term, it is argued, no correlation is visible between national development achievements and population growth rates. Mexico, with a rapidly growing population, has prospered, while Uruguay has combined slow population growth with economic stagnation.[7]

THE RURAL CRISIS

In Latin America, urban growth has not kept pace with the growth of rural areas. The urban environment is privileged compared to the rural zones: in Brazil the average income in the State of Guanabara (where Rio de Janeiro is located), is 10 times higher than in the rural state of Piau; in Venezuela the agricultural product is only 7.6 per cent of the average domestic product.[8]

Available data support estimates that the proportion of agricultural workers has been declining from 54.1 per cent in 1950 to 46.1 per cent in 1965, while continuing to grow in absolute numbers from 28.1 million in 1950 to 35.2 million in 1965.[9]

Living conditions in the rural environment present a heartrending picture. As the Rockefeller Report states: ". . . *campesino* goes to bed hungry every night of his life, he will probably never see a doctor, a hospital or a nurse." Conditions of sanitation, diet, education, and housing are deplorable.[10]

Despite a few innovations, agriculture remains out-of-date as a result of an inviolable "natural order."

Large landed estates predominate; combined with the small volume of investments in agriculture, they remain viable only by virtue of a closed stratification system and a primary system of labor relationships.

The rural stratification system perpetrates polarization and the poverty of the low rural class, whose income averages less than $100 (U.S.) per capita a year. The role played by the rural lower strata in the stagnation of the national economies has not been recognized, and in the discussion of rural living conditions, political or humanitarian considerations have predominated. The primary system of labor relationship precludes the contractual type. Rural life is based on direct bartering of services and even the exchange of favors. (Contractual relations between employers and workers are confined to those duties and rights which derive—directly and impersonally—from the payment of wages on the one hand and the fulfillment of the obligation to work on the other.) Manpower is recruited according to a system of loyalties which involves not only portions of a person's behavior and time but also covers his whole family. Therefore, a high percentage of employment of the active population in agriculture is associated with a higher percentage of unpaid family workers and children under 15, employed, but not paid, in agriculture. This non-contractual type of labor relation suggests that money plays a secondary role, if any, and it also suggests that individual merit or efficiency are not important organizational principles. Non-monetary methods of remuneration, traditional loyalties, dependence, and family labor are all factors unlikely to promote the profit motive.[11]

The day laborer, who occupies the lowest level in the peasant hierarchy, has no prospect of advancement. He has learned that his aspirations to land-ownership are hopeless, but he is still bound to it. The only way to resolve this contradiction is to work as well as to live in the large industrial city. What is most striking about this phenomenon, is—according to Lehman—that the peasant's life changes so little when he reaches the city.[12] Shanty towns, which are almost exclusively inhabited by peasants, preserve the traditions and the misery of the countryside, acting as buffers against the shock of the big city.

URBANIZATION

During the days of the pre-Columbian civilizations, as historians have pointed out, there were important urban centers which dominated huge areas of land and large agrarian populations. The Conquistadores and the early Spanish settlers were essentially urban in outlook, and whether using the Indian centers or founding new cities, their main concern was to establish administrative and commercial organization rather than to develop agricultural resources. This characteristic has persisted, causing the early growth of urban societies based mainly on foreign trade; consequently, Latin America's major cities are on the coast.

The concentration of income and consumption in the cities was centripetal; it lured human and financial resources away from the country. This imbalance limits agricultural production for urban consumption and deprives industry of rural markets, thus holding back the development of industry.

In the same way that imperial Spanish traditions accounted for the present tendency toward an absolute, centralized power in most of the Latin American nations (see Chapter 2), so an understanding of historical Spanish values will help us to understand industrial stagnation amidst uninterrupted urban growth:

> The sources of Latin American values have been generally credited to the institutions and names of the Iberian nations, as practiced by an Iberian-born elite during the three centuries of colonial rule. Those sent over from Spain or Portugal held the predominant positions, and in the colonies "ostentatiously proclaimed their lack of association with manual, productive labor or any kind of vile employment."
>
> Spain and Portugal, prior to colonizing the Americas, had been engaged for eight centuries in conflict with the Moors, resulting in the glorification of the roles of soldier and priest, and in the denigration of commercial and banking activities, often in the hands of Jews and Moslems. Iberian values were transferred to the American continent. To establish them securely, there were constant efforts by the "church militant" to christianize heathen population, the need to justify morally Spanish and Portuguese rule over inferior peoples, Indians, and imported Africans, and the fostering of the "get rich quick" mentality introduced by the *conquistadores*, but reinforced by efforts to locate valuable minerals or mine the land, and most significantly by the establishment of *latifundia* [large-scale plantations] as the predominant form of economic, social and political organization. . . . And in the Latin American scorn for pragmatism and materialism, now usually identified with the United States, there is an element that can only be explained by the existence of a traditional, landed upper class.[13]

Hence, the continuation of pre-industrial values in much of Latin America can be linked to the persistence of the social structure which originally fostered these values.

At present, urbanization is a process of concentration of population, of modernization of pre-existing urban patterns, and of diffusion of modern urban patterns to the whole population, including rural groups.

In Latin America this triple process is rapid and disruptive; it is predicted that at present trends, the largest cities will double their population every 14 years.[14]

This exceptional growth is due in part to the massive migration from the internal rural areas and small towns. Only in Argentina and Uruguay has urban predominance reached a level at which migration is not important. These are also the only countries in which agriculture has been regarded as a serious occupation.

Next to migration, the high rates of natural growth are responsible for the increasing percentages of the total population living in a few large cities of every country. A continuation of present trends in population growth and redistribution of this population will make the complex problems of urbanization even more unmanageable. The available techniques for urban planning seem useless and have been tacitly abandoned.[15]

All Latin America countries have a large percentage of recent migrants concentrated in a few cities; thus, Buenos Aires comprises 30 per cent of the total population of Argentina, and 10 per cent of the entire population of 20 Latin American countries is concentrated in only four cities: Buenos Aires, Rio de Janeiro, Sao Paulo, and Mexico City. Although many small and medium-sized cities exist in Latin America, opportunities for expanding and developing these cities as alternative centers for development are often overlooked.

The transition from rural norms, involving a high degree of social control, to urban norms, which means a comparative disintegration of social control, makes adjustment difficult for the migrant. The migrant enters an unformed environment where urban and rural values coexist. This mixture encourages the creation of subcultures. These subcultures are heavily influenced by radio, television, and cinema, which break down the traditional opposition to change and development, increasing at the same time the inner feeling of inequality and poverty.

This complex situation within major Latin American cities leads directly to the problems of inappropriate employment and housing and the so-called "marginalization."

UNEMPLOYMENT

The difficulties of adjusting to wage labor and industrial discipline, and the lack of industrial skills among newcomers to Latin American cities—especially among Indians—have aroused a keen interest in mitigating the undesirable effects that are now appearing in most cities.

D. Huenlin has noted that:

> All the major cities of Latin America are burdened with an unemployed and virtually unemployable population, inhabiting shanty towns and creating serious problems in matters of health, education and social services. . . . The influence of unemployed labor has been, and is, far in excess of the capacity of urban industry to absorb.[16]

Although urbanization in Latin America has proceeded independently of industrialization, the big cities are centers for the introduction, promotion, and dissemination of industrial goods. This creates needs that have been satisfied mostly by imports, and that have increased the sharp contrasts between urban and rural environments. At the same time, the importance of non-agricultural activities in towns is increasing. More families try to maintain themselves by petty commerce, selling goods and beverages, or working as watchmen, laundresses, domestic servants, and the like. For the majority, this is hardly more than a form of unemployment, but for a few it can mean the beginning of accumulation of capital and entry into a middle class.

While Latin American statistics on levels of employment and unemployment—and on the distribution of incomes and productivity within the different occupational categories—are insufficient, available data indicate that from 1950 to 1965 the percentage of those active in manufacturing has declined slightly, while the percentage in construction and basic services has increased moderately.

It may be expected that unemployment among migrants would rise to crisis levels.

> All these estimates mean that the worker, and especially the factory worker, is comparatively privileged and isolated within a population which lives off marginal activities.[17]

HOUSING

Next to employment, housing is the most difficult single problem of the urban poor. Construction industries are oriented to the upper-income strata. In general, housing conditions in Latin America are extremely poor and steadily deteriorating.

Most striking is the spread of large shanty towns; for example, the population in the *favelas* in Rio de Janeiro reached 1 million in 1961, representing 30 per cent of the city's total population. In the Colombian city of Buenaventura, 80 per cent of the population lives in *tuqurios*. In Peru, the population of *barriadas* in Lima grew from 10 per cent in 1940 to 21 per cent in 1960. In other countries, these slums or shanty towns are called *conventillos, rancherias, villas miserias, colonias proletarias,* and are constanly increasing in number and size.

It is known that 45 per cent of the urban and 50 per cent of the rural dwellers are now living in inadequate housing, defined as "buildings that are not in keeping with human dignity and that should be demolished."[18] At least 30 per cent of the housing units in the primary cities lacked running water, electricity, and main drains in 1960.

Millions of Latin Americans live with no assurance of remaining in the same place from day to day. Some of them have no homes at all, but find temporary shelter in the streets, under bridges, or with other crowded households. In addition, most of the dwellings that are passable today will become unusable in the next 20 or 30 years.

Shanty towns that fringe the burgeoning industrial cities are like open sores, usually within smelling distance of the prosperous sections; but the toll of rural misery is a hidden shame. The home of the farmer or villager is flimsy and lacks minimal hygienic facilities.

Building homes means building communities, and before people can work together for urban decency, they must acquire a feeling of community.[19] The number of dwelling units required to house the Latin American urban population will be, according to the U.N., 33.4 million by 1975, and for rural areas 32.3 million.

Housing needs, expressed in dwellings per 1,000 population, ranges from 14.1 in 1960 to 10.8 in 1975, a rate of output which exceeds anything so far achieved.

Only in Chile, Colombia, and Costa Rica is there an increase in residential building which coincides with the initiation of national housing programs oriented toward low- and minimum-cost housing.[20]

MARGINALITY AND MARGINALIZATION[21]

Rising proportions of Latin American population are undergoing new and distressing socio-economic changes. Rural workers dominated by the patronage and the *hacienda* systems were not marginal, however poor and excluded from national life they might have been, nor were self-sufficient farmers and tribesmen. Neither are urban workers marginal to the extent that they have access to regular employment and are able to advance their interests through their own organizations. Marginality refers to the growth of strata in close contact with the national economies and societies, under multiple stimuli to participate in them, but able to do so only marginally.[22]

Traditional occupations are decreasingly able to afford them a livelihood, while communications media urge them to increase consumption and political movements inform them of rights to a more adequate level of living. Increasing poverty, whether absolute or in terms of the widening gap between felt needs and incomes; increasing insecurity of employment; community and family ties; shelter; ability to cope with problems; and increasing geographical and occupational mobility go together. The last of these trends means that the phenomenon of marginality in urban and rural settings is becoming increasingly similar.

It is probable that at least 25 per cent of the population in Latin American cities is now living in marginal settlements and that this population is growing considerably faster than the rest of the urban population, at rates between 10 and 15 per cent annually. If these trends continue, the irregular settlements will eventually contain a majority of the population.

At the same time, reasons can be found for hope that marginality is not equivalent to a self-perpetuating vicious circle of poverty, that the marginal strata can become constructive participants in the evolution of new societies.

As long as the cities were small and the rural majorities were controlled and isolated by the *hacienda* or their own community, the obvious inadequacies did not stimulate real demands exerting pressure on the public sector. The demands are now real and potentially overwhelming, coming from the much larger rural and urban strata that have previously received only token benefits from public social action, mainly in the forms of a year or two of elementary schooling and some protection against communicable disease. Urbanization, by coinciding with the breakdown of the security of religion and ancestral loyalties, has catalyzed new trends which are changing the meaning of deficient social services.

NOTES

1. Horowitz, I. L., *Three Worlds of Development, the Theory and Practice of International Stratification,* New York, Oxford University Press, 1966.

2. Lipset, S. M., *Elites in Latin America,* New York, Oxford University Press, 1967, p. 34.

3. U.N., *1967 World Social Situation,* pp. 130–31.

4. U.N., *1963 Report on the World Social Situation,* p. 123.

5. Miro, Carmen A., "The Population of Latin America," in *Latin America and the Caribbean, A Handbook,* Claudio Veliz (Ed.), pp. 666–73.

6. These percentages reflect the most recent census. Source: U.N., *1967 Report on the World Social Situation, loc. cit.*

7. *Ibid.,* p. 128.

8. *Ibid.,* p. 126, Table 1.

9. *Ibid.,* p. 138.

10. *The Rockefeller Report on the Americas,* Chicago, Quadrangle Books, 1969, p. 131.

11. U.N., *Social Development of Latin America in the Post-War Period,* pp. 21–51.

12. Lehman, D., "The Agrarian Working Class," in *Latin America and the Caribbean, A Handbook,* Claudio Veliz (Ed.), p. 688.

13. Lipset, *op. cit.,* p. 8.

14. U.N., *1963 Report on the World Social Situation,* p. 123.

15. U.N., *1967 Report on the World Social Situation,* p. 131.

16. Huenlin, D., "Latin America: a Summary of Economic Problems," in *Latin America and the Caribbean, A Handbook,* Claudio Veliz (Ed.), p. 469.

17. Pecant, D., "The Urban Working Class," *ibid.,* pp. 674–80.

18. U.N., *World Housing Conditions and Estimated Housing Requirements,* New York, 1969, pp. 26–34.

19. Maury, M., *The Good War,* New York, Macfadden Publications, 1965, pp. 134–41.

20. U.N., *1967 Report on the World Social Situation,* p. 53.

21. *Ibid.,* pp. 140–42.

22. cp. Toynbee: ". . . our definition of 'internal proletariat' has been psychological, we have used it to denote those who felt that they no longer 'belonged' to the society within which they found themselves included physically." In A. J. Toynbee, *A Study of History,* abridged by D. C. Somervell, N.Y., Oxford University Press, 1957, Vol. 2, p. 316.

CHAPTER 5

The Organization and Planning of Social Programs

SOCIAL SECURITY

IN all 20 Latin American countries, social security systems are suffering from inadequate financing, administrative hypertrophy, and inequities in benefits, coverage of rural workers, especially, being woefully insufficient.

Old age, invalidism, indigent survivors, illness and medical needs, maternity, unemployment, problems which are likely to arise in the agricultural sector, occur also in the industrial sector, and probably more frequently. The problem is further compounded by the fact that the migrant worker may have left a subsistence agricultural sector in which barter arrangements were more important than money transactions. Thus, when he enters into an employment relationship, he relinquishes his former independence and perhaps self-reliance and exchanges his labor for money rather than for goods in kind. An urban resident must make cash payments for food, shelter, clothing, and health care. Savings dwindle and reliance on other family members or on relatives may not be sufficient or forthcoming.

Social security is important in facilitating rural to urban migration and in lessening the social costs which arise from the process of industrialization, but social security protection in the urbanizing area is incomplete. Also, the real value of pensions and other benefits may decline in the face of inflation. The beneficiaries give vent to their frustration under these circumstances. A number of countries have already undertaken comprehensive reform.[1]

EDUCATION

In spite of high rates of illiteracy among the population aged 15 years or over,[2] upward trends in education have attained a momentum. Between 1956 and 1965, for Latin America as a whole, the percentage of the total population enrolled in schools of some kind rose from 13.3 to 17.1. This gain reflects an average annual rate of increase of 7.2 per cent, about 2½ times the regional rate of population increase. The share of public expenditure on education also increased.[3] However, the problems of retardation and waste remained as serious as ever. The duration of attendance at the average primary school in Latin America is 2.2 years.[4]

The average age at which children enter school and their success at school is closely related to the special and economic status of their parents. In 1957, 41 per cent of primary enrollment was concentrated in the first grade, only 7 per cent in the highest primary grade. In 1965, the percentages were 38 and 8. In secondary schooling there is evidence that dropout rates are higher. Some universities, with considerably increased enrollments, are turning out no more graduates than before.[5] The educationl systems are criticized for not making a contribution to the increases needed in economic production. Teaching methods tend to be oral and expositive and encourage memorizing and repetition. Failure rates are high and examinations rely on feedback from texts.

Trapp has pointed out that:

> The mediocre education provided to the majority of the peasant and urban lower class population in Latin America seems to do little except offer them a fleeting acquaintance with literacy and to be useless in economic terms. . . . It has been estimated that between a third and a half of the children born and raised in the countryside will move to the towns and seek urban employment. Throughout Latin America, the towns are suffering from a shortage of skilled workers and a growing surplus of completely unskilled rural migrants. Education would best therefore train the rural child both for continued life in the countryside and also for the new task of urban-industrial employment.[6]

Secondary education is concentrated almost entirely on preparation for the universities, but an increasing number of students are unable to attend a university. Reforms aiming at diversification of the secondary school system have not yet penetrated the system to any great extent.

It has been said that rural education is a wasteful and pathetically ineffective imitation of urban education, and urban education in turn imitates the academic education meant to cultivate the mind of a leisured elite.

THE UNIVERSITY

In the universities, there is—according to one report from the U.N.—a ". . . strange combination of ideological ferment and organizational paralysis that has resulted from the contradictory pressures on them."[7]

The preference for the traditional careers of law and medicine and the lack of technical schools at an intermediary level is cited by Horowitz as an example of the obsolete pattern of superior education, oriented toward individual prestige and promotion within a rigid class system and not toward the problems of technical and economical development.[8]

In Argentina, which is a basically agricultural country, only 1.9 per cent of the university students are enrolled in agriculture, while 33.7 per cent are in medicine and 13 per cent in law. In Brazil, 3.9 per cent of the students are majoring in agriculture, 16.4 per cent are in medicine, and 21.8 are in law.[9]

Furthermore, there is a tendency to give to the students a rigid body of knowledge which has to be learned by rote, leaving the professional unprepared to face problems not discussed in his textbooks. In this environment research is not possible and the concept of modernization, instead of investigating national problems, concentrates on imitating solutions which have worked in developed and modern countries. Students in medicine, for example, will restrict their practices to the higher strata of the society, while the majority of the population will take recourse in *curranderos* and quacks.[10] Physicians receive a particular pride in their knowledge from the university that interferes with the idea of descending to help the lower strata. Also, their models and sources of security are increasingly those from abroad, so the increasing emigration of graduate professionals is another consequence of this situation.

This outflow means that a significant part of Latin American educational investment benefits other regions (the "brain drain").[11] The inability of Latin American countries to retain the cream of their labor forces is further complicated by a lack of well-defined demands for professionals as well as poor salaries and working conditions. For example, doctors are badly needed, but the number that can be supported by market demands is less than the number available.[12]

PUBLIC HEALTH

It is probable that the rise in life expectancies and lower mortality rates are continuing, but that rates of change are slowing down as control of communicable diseases increases, while widening coverage by public health services encounters the limitations imposed by low—even deteriorating—nutritional and living standards. The diseases spread by polluted water are now the leading causes of death in many Latin American countries and are serious in practically all of them. The provision of sanitation facilities to urban low-income zones, small towns, and villages constitutes an important and relatively expensive further stage in the struggle against diseases.

Public health services absorb sizable percentages of central government expenditure in most countries, ranging from 16.2 in Peru and 14.9 in Mexico to 2.8 in Bolivia and 4.1 in Paraguay;[13] but the expansion of resources seems to have been relatively limited. The remarkable increase in life expectancies—in Mexico up from 50 years in 1950 to 66 in 1965, with other countries showing increases of eight years or more[14]—has not meant appreciable change in age distribution because of continuing high fertility. However, the fact that large numbers of persons of all ages are now surviving under unfavorable conditions means that pressures for a wide range of modern medical services, from the pediatric to the geriatric, are bound to rise rapidly.

What is more important is a general deficiency of health service personnel. Furthermore, the facilities for training doctors and other health service workers—nurses, midwives, auxiliary personnel, technicians—are often inadequate. The doctor/population ratio is now considered the best indicator of the national availability of health services. This ratio ranges from 1 doctor to 670 population in Argentina, which is one of the highest in the world, to 1 to 14,200 in Haiti.[15]

However, hospitals and physicians tend to concentrate in larger cities, and there is a lag in organizing and staffing clinics in rural and urban marginal areas. Paradoxically, there are developed countries which regard a doctor/population ratio of 1 to 750 as hardly sufficient for their present needs, and certain to be inadequate in the future, as the techniques of modern medicine become more demanding.[16] This need will attract numerous doctors from the poor countries, for the richer nations offer incomparably superior remuneration. Such a situation poses a real dilemma for the planning of health in developing countries, either independently or with international assistance.

SOCIAL DISEASES

It may be difficult to state exactly what constitutes a social disease. However, if we regard the definition as covering diseases and occurrences which have as one of their contributory etiological factors some social variables which can be manipulated, a number of the health problems of Latin America probably qualify.

Malnutrition, mainly because of its association with poverty, is a social disease. As a social phenomenon it can be alleviated, but not cured, by scientific research and the application of scientific discoveries. It also requires aid in personnel and finance.[17] The most active step taken so far has been the establishment of the Institute of Nutrition for Central America and Panama (INCAP).

Polluted water and defective sanitation are also obviously related to social and economic development and are strongly influenced by rapid urbanization and industrialization. Akin to the question of urbanization is that of population pressure; however, planned parenthood remains suspect to many Latin Americans. All the Latin American countries risk being overwhelmed by a miasma of physical misery and disease if urgent action is not promptly initiated.

Other conditions with origins in the social background of modern life are venereal diseases and prostitution, alcoholism, narcotic addiction, and crime, all of which share a number of etiological factors such as population movements, urbanization, industrialization, economic affluence, and changing behavior patterns. Control of these problems can no longer be left to the clinic or isolated agencies; a combined operation in which specialized agencies cooperate with national governments and international organizations is necessary. As a recent report from the United Nations has pointed out:

> Efforts to accelerate economic growth and promote higher living standards have at the same time created problems of adjustments for certain groups. . . . However . . . there seems to be insufficient awareness of the implication of these burgeoning social problems and a tendency to neglect them. . . . Urban-rural imbalances, which accompany the movements of people between country and town, result in the unhealthy growth of urban communities. . . .

Experience has shown the overall impact of such unbalance on children and young people has, in some cases, manifested itself in juvenile criminality (and prostitution and alcoholism). The expansion of education, for example, has created problems of adjustment for some children and young adults. Unemployment among school dropouts is cumulative as each year increases the number of idle youths in relation to the number of available jobs. Semi-educated dropouts tend to reject agriculture and seek, usually unsuccessfully, white collar jobs. Those who complete the courses are not necessarily more successful . . . those with unfulfilled aspirations are likely to turn their energies to illegitimate ends. The emergence and increase of juvenile delinquency in Latin America and other developing countries is particularly noted in rapidly expanding urban areas.[18]

NOTES

1. U.N., *1967 Report on the World Social Situation,* pp. 87–88 and 147–48.

2. According to the U.N. (*Social Development of Latin America in the Post-War Period,* p. 43), the percentages of the total illiterate population are: Argentina, 14; Bolivia, 68; Brazil, 53; Chile, 23; Colombia, 48; Costa Rica, 23; Cuba, 23; Dominican Republic, 38; Ecuador, 44; El Salvador, 64; Guatemala, 75; Haiti, 89; Honduras, 65; Mexico, 58; Nicaragua, 63; Panama, 33; Paraguay, 33; and Venezuela, 48.

3. U.N., *1967 Report on the World Social Situation,* pp. 143–44.

4. Trapp, A., "Education," in *Latin America and the Caribbean, A Handbook,* Claudio Veliz (Ed.), pp. 712–19.

5. U.N., *1967 Report on the World Social Situation,* p. 144.

6. Trapp, *loc. cit.*

7. U.N., *1967 Report on the World Social Situation,* p. 145.

8. Horowitz, I. L., *Three Worlds of Development, the Theory and Practice of International Stratification,* New York, Oxford University Press, 1966, p. 354.

9. Naciones Unidas, *Educacion, recursos humanos y desarrollo en America Latina,* 1968, p. 119.

10. *Ibid.,* p. 155.

11. U.N., *1967 Report on the World Social Situation,* p. 145.

12. U.N., *1965 Report on the World Social Situation,* pp. 62–64.

13. U.N., *1967 Report on the World Social Situation,* p. 126, Table 1.

14. The average life span is 57 years for Latin America. In the U.S. it is 70 years (*The Rockefeller Report . . . ,* p. 131).

15. According to the third report on the World Health Situation (World Health Organization, 1967), the doctor/population ratio for each of the Latin American countries is Argentina, 1/670; Bolivia, 1/3,700; Brazil, 1/2000; Chile, 1/2300; Colombia, 1/2,025; Costa Rica, 1/2,560; Cuba,

1/1,210; Dominican Republic, 1/1,600; Ecuador, 1/5,200; El Salvador, 1/4,700; Guatemala, 1/3,660; Haiti, 1/4,200; Honduras, 1/9,250; Mexico, 1/1,800; Nicaragua, 1/2,800; Panama, 1/2,400; Paraguay, 1/1,700; Peru, 1/2,200; Uruguay, 1/880; and Venezuela, 1/1,300.

16. *Ibid.,* p. 60.
17. *Ibid.,* p. 58.
18. U.N., *1967 Report on the World Social Situation,* p. 104.

CHAPTER 6

Mental Health

PSYCHIATRIC SERVICES

IN the first chapter, we pointed out a greater emphasis throughout the world on the social aspects of psychiatry compared with the clinical approach. Horowitz said in 1962 that ". . . the attitude of the Latin American society towards the prevention of mental illness has not been substantially changed since 400 years ago."[1] Nevertheless, the preoccupation with the problems of mental disorders has always been present in Latin America. The pre-Columbian civilization of the Andes and Mexico had a special law to control a number of manifestations of psychiatric illness. Archaeological discoveries have led Calderon Narvaez, a Mexican psychiatrist, to affirm that:

> Due to alcohol problems, these cultures [Toltecs, Mayas, and Aztecs] dictated several laws to restrain consumption. . . . When the Spaniards suppressed these laws, the aborigines increased the consumption of alcohol tremendously.[2]

In 1566 a psychiatric hospital was opened in Mexico, but at the end of the eighteenth century there was only one other in Quito,

Ecuador. With the independence movement in the nineteenth century, the ideas of Pinel and Esquirol were introduced into Latin America and psychiatric hospitals arose in most of the important cities of the region. However, not until 1956—when a psychiatric hospital was opened in Honduras—did all the Latin American countries have such institutions.[3]

In 1957, there were 237 psychiatric hospitals with about 100,000 beds for the 20 Latin American nations.[4] There were 3,500 psychiatrists or physicians working in the field of psychiatry and mental health.[5] There is an extreme disparity in the distribution of psychiatric facilities and manpower. One-half of the total beds in Latin America as a whole are concentrated in Brazil, and almost one-half of the psychiatrists in Argentina. Moreover, hospitals and psychiatrists are located in the major cities and there are no specialized services in the rural and marginal zones. Of all the Latin American psychiatrists, 28 per cent are living in one city: Buenos Aires. The psychiatrist/population ratio, estimated from a list of the Pan American Health Organization,[6] is 1 psychiatrist per 75,000 population for Latin America as a whole, ranging from 1 psychiatrist per 16,000 in Argentina to 1 per 500,000 in Bolivia. While the World Health Organization considers that ". . . it is necessary to provide one bed for mental patients per 1,000 population," this ratio for Latin America as a whole is less than .55 per 1,000 and only four countries have a ratio near 1 to 1,000: Argentina (1.24), Panama (1.17), Uruguay (1.06), and Costa Rica (.95). The lowest ratios are those of Haiti, with .08 beds per 1,000 population, and Peru and Bolivia, with .11.[7]

Mexico, the first country to have a psychiatric hospital in the Americas, has also been the first to build new hospitals in accordance with the architectural and technological requirements of modern psychiatry. Since the beginning of 1965, a new complex of model hospitals has been set up, with 2,000 new beds, which offer the latest therapeutic and rehabilitative care, on a short- or a long-term basis, with the facilities to train the necessary staff and ancillary personnel.[8] The poorer countries cannot afford showplace buildings; thus, better use of the resources already at hand has begun to replace the former insistence on larger, more elaborate resources among mental health planners. For example, in Honduras there is only one psychiatric hospital, with insufficient material and human resources. To remedy this situation one of the solutions proposed was to build a new psychiatric hospital on the outskirts of Tegucigalpa; however, a study sponsored by the Pan American Health Organization concluded that building a new hospital was bound to fail, especially because of the shortage of staff and money. Promotion of modern therapies and work to be carried out in close cooperation with general medical centers were recommended. The present psychiatric hospital should be used to a greater extent for educational purposes, so that even with the modest financial means available, professionals might be trained in brief and intensive courses on psychiatric techniques for use in cities located far from the capital.[9]

SOCIAL PSYCHIATRY

With the development of chemotherapy, many psychiatric disorders can now be successfully treated, and therapeutic programs are becoming more practical and prestigious. Consequently, by 1970 a growing concern was evident about the problems created by the present conditions of life. "Adjustment" is now seen as a two-way process—while individuals must make certain adaptation to the society in which they live, the social structure must also adapt to their changing needs and aspirations. Social psychiatry is concerned with both kinds of adjustment.

> For each society, and for each segment of society within which the psychiatrist finds his patients, he is able to provide new insights which, when translated with the help of educators and social scientists, become preventive measures to provide for the better [adjustment and] mental health of future generations. But the psychiatrist's practice must be local, it is not possible to go from the psychiatrist's insight in a large Parisian hospital to a Latin American plantation.[10]

Slowly but surely there has developed an almost universal appreciation of the role that psychology and psychiatry can play, not only in alleviating the personal troubles of individuals, but also in providing an approach to the solution of the problems of the modern world.[11]

Because of new and wider demands concerning prevention, treatment, and rehabilitation of mental disorders in masses of people who hitherto have remained out of the sight of psychiatrists, this new type of specialist, who requires changes in the traditional methods of medical training, is said to suffer from a "crisis of professional identity" in settings in which the demand for psychiatry is far from clearcut or dependable. Thus there is a growing tendency to integrate mental care services with those for other illnesses. Evidence of this is the use of general hospitals as psychiatric wards and out-patient clinics. The prime example of this move is Costa Rica, where more than half the number of beds for psychiatric patients are found in general hospitals, 885 out of a total of 1.566.[12] In Asuncion, Paraguay, there is a mental health clinic where psychiatric disorders are treated in a general medical center, sharing the same organization, services, and waiting-room; the success of this clinic can be seen in the increase in the number of patients seeking a first interview: from 247 patients in 1959 to 690 in 1966.[13]

Other countries have placed great reliance on community care, operating in association with the social services as a supplement, if not replacement, for institutional treatment. The advantages are considerable both for the patient and the responsible health authority. This kind of approach has been reported as one of the goals of a project for an *Unidad de Salud Mental* (Mental Health Unit) in Santiago de Chile.[14]

The Pilot Plan of Social Psychiatry in Cali, Colombia, to be described in the forthcoming pages, uses the existing facilities and personnel of public health services, which have been functioning for community care of mental patients since July 1967.

PSYCHIATRIC EPIDEMIOLOGY

Epidemiological studies are scarce in Latin America. There is in general little information regarding the prevalence and incidence of mental illness; this situation is compounded by the obvious shortage and inadequate distribution of staff trained in the scientific methodology required for such studies. Methodological difficulties seriously hinder any attempt to evaluate the magnitude and intensity of mental disorders in population groups.

The identification of mental illness and the computation of specific morbidity rates are performed only in a few Latin American countries, and without any agreement about the classification and taxonomy; in fact, Leon has found a remarkable resistance, among psychiatrists of 19 Latin American nations, to discuss the classification of mental disorders.[15] This lack of common classification defeats any attempt to compare psychiatric observations and the results of treatment undertaken in the various countries.

Deaths caused by alcoholism, homicide, and suicide illustrate a public health problem closely related to psychiatry. In Guatemala 6.2 per 100,000 population died because of alcoholism in 1955, and 3.3 per 100,000 in both Chile and Costa Rica. In Santiago de Chile, from 1947 to 1955, more than 25 per cent of the admissions to one psychiatric hospital were due to alcoholism.[16]

Homicide in Colombia reached a rate of 48 per 100,000 in 1958 and 40 per 100,000 in 1960. In Mexico and El Salvador these rates were more than 30 per 100,000 in 1960, which is high compared with homicide rates in other countries: 4.6 per 100,000 in the U.S., 1.7 in Peru, and 1.4 in Canada for 1960.[17]

Suicide, on the other hand, is a phenomenon which is increasing day by day in Venezuela. Death by suicide was in 22nd place in 1964 and in 15th place in 1967 (the rate was 6.3 per 100,000 in 1965). The rates of suicide in Latin American countries during 1965 range from 11.3 per 100,000 in El Salvador to .9 per 100,000 in the Dominican Republic and .6 in Ecuador.[18]

Suicide rates are higher in the major cities and higher among men than women. In eight cities, Bogotá, Cali, La Plata, Lima, Mexico City, Riberao Preto, Sao Paulo, and Caracas, the figures oscillated between 12.8 and 20.8 for men (in Santiago de Chile higher than 30) during the period 1962–1964. For women in the same cities and years, the figures were between 5.1 and 12.1.

The most common methods of suicide were poisoning, hanging, shooting, and jumping from high places. Poisoning was the method used most often by women. They used insecticides and raticides in Bogotá, Caracas, Cali, Lima, and Sao Paulo, and barbiturates in Mexico City.

There are no specialized centers for the study and prevention of suicide, and in most Latin American countries the records that do exist are unreliable. Because of the difficulties involved in obtaining reliable information from mortality data and hospital records, it is advisable to refer to field surveys. These are essential for assessing needs for psychiatric care in a specific society and for uncovering clues about etiology.

FIELD SURVEYS

In Latin American there have been very few field surveys which meet the requirements of epidemiological methodology. Some examples will be cited.

Leon, in a prevalence study of mental disorders in El Cerrito, Colombia, arrived at the conclusion that the proportion of individuals in need of psychiatric treatment did not differ greatly from those in Bristol, Canada, and was almost identical to the proportion found in Manhattan in previous studies.[19] In another prevalence study in an urban area (El Guabal, Colombia), the same author reached the conclusion that the prevalence rate of psychosis, which was 25 per 1,000, did not differ significantly from the prevalence rates of mental disturbances in 12 different countries with an average of 28.6 per 1,000.[20] Yet another study, carried out in Lima by Mariategui, revealed the following figures: neurosis, 5.4 per cent; personality disturbances, 3.4 per cent; psychiatric disturbances in children, 3.1 per cent; alcoholism, 2.7 per cent; convulsions, 1.4 per cent; mental deficiency, 1.4 per cent; psychophysiological disturbances, 1.2 per cent; and psychosis, 1.2 per cent.

Personality disturbances were common in men and, as with alcoholism, were more frequently found in "independent" rather than in passive and dependent personalities. Alcoholism, mental deficiency, and mental disturbances in children appeared in lower classes more frequently than expected. On the other hand, psychophysiological disturbances were more common in middle classes.[21]

In Chile, it has been estimated that 20 per cent of the population has psychiatric problems.[22] A study carried out in Lima by

Munoz-Bautista showed that about 30 per cent of the population suffered from some kind of psychiatric disturbance, and that this was more pronounced in adolescents and young adults.[23] In Buenos Aires, Fontanarossa found centroencephalic epilepsy disorders in the electro-encephalographic charts of most children with learning difficulties. Children with this disorder were generally not treated psychiatrically.[24]

In Honduras, Hudgens undertook a transcultural study comparing the diagnostic distribution and phenomenology of mental diseases treated in a hospital in Tegucigalpa, with samples from a private U.S. hospital (the Renard Hospital) and another public institution in St. Louis (the Malcolm Bliss Center), using standardized interviews and diagnostic criteria. Despite geographical, cultural, racial, religious, and economic differences between the inhabitants of Tegucigalpa and St. Louis, he reported the same psychiatric disorders in both cities. In fact, he recommended that special attention be given to diagnostic criteria in any transcultural research work, and also suggested that the basic treatment methods that have proven to be effective in one country will also be useful in another, even if the latter has a different culture.[25]

Men who suffer from depressive symptoms in Honduras usually resort to alcohol, whereas women prefer to seek help from witchdoctors or doctors. The suicide rate in 1963 was 3.8 per cent per 100,000 persons in Honduras (4.5 men and 3 per cent women). These figures are debatable, however, because of the difference in the concentration of doctors in the various areas of the country. It was also found that 12 per cent of the interviews carried out in Honduras showed a history of suicide attempts, compared to 11 per cent of the Renard Hospital patients. Moreover, 23 per cent of the group from Honduras admitted having intended to commit suicide, against only 16 per cent of the Renard Hospital group. It is true that the indicated rate represents only one-fourth or one-fifth of the suicide rate in the United States, but the aforementioned findings make this statement uncertain.

In general terms, it was found that in the three hospitals under consideration, functional psychosis prevailed among hospitalized patients, and that in the outpatient clinic, 31 per cent of the patients suffered from depression and 30 per cent from epilepsy.

The paucity of these examples makes it impossible to arrive at final conclusions, but it is possible to say that the magnitude of the mental health problems in the population of various areas of Latin America is at least equal to that of other, more developed, countries. Moreover, the overwhelming scarcity of studies and services makes it well-nigh impossible to set up even the most elementary psychiatric care programs, and this scarcity is even worse in comparison to the developed regions. Presumably, mental health has low priority in the scale of needs and demands of developing countries.

NOTES

1. Horwitz, A., "Propositos y Provecciones del Seminario Latinoamericano de Salud Mental," Oficina Panamericana de Salud (OPS), *Publicacion Cientifica No. 81,* 1963, p. 3.

2. Calderon, Narvaez G., "Consideraciones Acerca del Alcoholismo entre los Pueblos Pre-Hispanicos de Mexico," *Revista del Instituto Nacional de Neurologia,* Vol. ii, No. 3, 1968, pp. 5–13.

3. Velasco, Alzaga J., "La Salud Mental en Las Americas," *Primer Seminario Latinoamericano de Salud Mental,* OPS, *Publicacion Cientifica No. 81,* 1963, pp. 8–28.

4. *Ibid.*

5. O.P.S., "Directory of Psychiatrists in Latin America," *Publicacion Cientifica No. 163,* 1968.

6. *Ibid.*

7. Horwitz, J., "Epidemiologia de los Problemas de Salud Mental," OPS, *Publicacion Cientifica No. 81,* 1963, pp. 29–37.

8. Calderon, Narvaez G., *Las Instituciones Hospitalarias y Su Importancia en la Asistencia Psiquiatrica,* V Congreso, Association Psiquiatrica de America Latina (APAL), Bogotá, 1968 (mimeograph).

9. Hudgens, R. W., *Mental Health Services in a Developing Country, Achievements and Obstacles in the Public Psychiatric Programs of Honduras,* Tegucigalpa, 1968 (mimeograph).

10. Mead, Margaret (Ed.), *Cultural Patterns and Technical Change,* New York, Mentor Books, UNESCO, 1955, p. 266.

11. WHO, *Third Report on the World Health Situation,* p. 126.

12. Calderon, Narvaez G., *Las Instituciones Hospitalarias,* 1968.

13. Carrizosa, A. *et al., Asistencia Psiquiatrica desde una Clinica de Salud Mental en un Centro de Salud, Asuncion, Paraguay,* V Congreso APAL, Bogotá, 1968 (mimeograph).

14. Munoz, L. C., Horwitz, J., and Marconi, J., "Programa de Trabajo de una Unidad de Salud Mental en Santiago de Chile," *Boletin de la Asociacion Psiquiatrica de America Latina,* Ano 1, No. 2, 1968.

15. Leon, C. A., *Actitudes de los Psiquiatras Latinoamericanos hacia la*

Clasificacion de Trastornos Mentales, V Congreso APAL, Bogotá, 1968 (mimeograph).

16. Data about alcoholism in Chile: Horwitz, *op. cit.*

17. Rates of deaths by alcoholism and homicide are taken from Velazco Alzaga, *op. cit.*

18. Sources of data about suicide in Venezuela and other Latin American countries from Rendon, R., *Epidemiological Aspects of Suicide and Attempted Suicide in Venezuela,* Caracas, 1969 (mimeograph).

19. Leon, C. A. *et al., Evaluacion de Instrumentos para el Estudio de Prevalencia de Trastornos Mentales,* V Congreso APAL, Bogotá, 1968 (mimeograph).

20. Leon, C. A., *Prevalencia de Trastornos Mentales en un Sector Urbano de Cali,* VI Congreso Colombiano de Psiquiatria, Pasto, 1966.

21. Mariategui, J. *et al., Prevalencia de Desordenes Mentales en un Distrito Urbano de Lima,* V Congreso APAL, Bogotá, 1968 (mimeograph).

22. Munoz, L. C., Horwitz, J., and Marconi, J., *loc. cit.*

23. Munoz Bautista, C., *Epidemiologia Neuropsiquiatrica en Adolecentes y adultos Jovenes,* V Congreso APAL, Bogotá, 1968 (mimeograph).

24. Fontanarossa, H. *et al., Distorsion de la Relacion entre el Nina Epileptico y el Grupo Familiar,* V Congreso APAL, Bogotá, 1968 (mimeograph).

25. Hudgens, R. W. *et al., Psychiatric Illness in a Developing Country: A Clinical Study of 227 Inpatients and 419 Outpatients in Honduras,* Tegucigalpa, 1968 (mimeograph).

CHAPTER **7**

Psychiatry
and the Problems
of Development

THE POPULATION PROBLEM

BESIDES the awareness of the "population problem" as a cause of economic and social difficulties[1] a psychiatrist in Latin America must accept the fact that the age structure offers a unique opportunity for preventive work with children and early treatment of the problems of childhood and youth. One of the disorders that can benefit from preventive psychiatry in a population with the age structure of Latin America is the "maternal deprivation" syndrome which manifests symptoms of mental retardation, personality defects, and social maladaptation, and which can be observed in children who may or may not also have a detectable central nervous system impairment.[2] According to Eisenberg, this syndrome could be considered endemic in most of the underdeveloped countries of the world because of its multiple causal factors which start even before conception in maternal poor health and in parental unreadiness for child rearing, coupled with the unavailability of birth control methods. The next assault comes during pregnancy and parturition.[3]

After birth the biological hazard becomes severe through malnutrition and specific nutritional deficiencies, accidents, and infections which may impair the central nervous system.

However serious the neuropathological sequelae of maldevelopment, malnutrition, injury, and infection, they are no more fateful than the psychopathologic sequelae of the intellectual understimulation, noxious interpersonal experiences, and social psychopathy to which these children are exposed. Far too many contribute to disease statistics, and they become premature and inadequate parents themselves, fated to repeat the cycle of deprivation.

PROBLEMS OF URBANIZATION AND INDUSTRIALIZATION

As in almost all the countries of the world at present, in Latin America man is going through startling changes. Never before has so much been required of the human being.[4] Migration to the city means homelessness for thousands who live in close physical proximity, separated from village ways, in a climate of alienation and insecurity. The consequence is the lack of any feeling of community.[5] Only a step removed from them in misfortune are other millions whose rural or tribal traditions provide them with stable social relationships but whose extreme poverty condemns them to live in subhuman conditions. In the overcrowded cities, the collective atmosphere makes it impossible for the human being to feel at home: he becomes an anonymous element. Deprived of emotional and intellectual satisfactions arising from his belonging to a community, normal adaptation is disrupted and mental or emotional disorder can result. Then the new urbanites, and even the traditional old-fashioned city dwellers, are pushed into technological work where human relations must be impersonal, where they must not become deep relations. But even so, those who finally get factory jobs are better off than those who remain unemployed and potentially unemployable because they lack skills. All these problems are exacerbated by the population explosion, malnutrition, illiteracy, and political upheavals.

We still do not know the ultimate effects of these transformations on the human being, but it can be said that present living conditions are harmful physically and psychologically. It is almost certain that malnutrition—and especially the lack of protein—impairs mental capabilities even before birth. The same thing is assumed with regard to the scarcity of stimulation caused by illiteracy and poor housing. We already mentioned how unemployment seems to be directly related to the increasing rates of crime and alcoholism (see Chapter 5). Political instability can be blamed for a lot of anxiety, depression, and family disharmony. These problems cannot be solved by psychiatrists, but they can help them. Furthermore, psychiatric knowledge of adaptive capabilities could help make change less disruptive and eventually oriented toward social improvement and individual adjustment.

PSYCHIATRY AND THE LOWER CLASSES

In Latin America, huge masses of people live at the level of mere subsistence. Only a very few elite groups and the small urban middle classes escape poverty.

Latin American lower classes share some features which must be considered when planning innovations in the field of mental health. Besides poverty, they are under the stresses of swift and radical social change. Also, they do not belong to the Western technological culture. These three conspicuous characteristics are too often overlooked by Western-minded psychiatrists.

A psychiatrist facing urban or rural lower-class patients often confronts totally different values and ethics, as well as a lack of enthusiasm over such incentives as a higher income or a more hygienic dwelling. These unexpected and, for him, illogical or aberrant responses leads him describe the psychological traits of peasants and newcomers to the marginal barrios in terms of psychopathic, asocial, anti-social, and immature personalities, thus evoking some ambiguous genetic or constitutional disorder. The theory of a socio-cultural etiology is now used to explain those psychological traits.

Anthropologists and sociologists have described elsewhere a "culture of the poor," and the term "culture of poverty" has become popular since it was first used by Oscar Lewis in 1961.[6] Some of the characteristics of the poor are, according to Brotman, 1) a cognitive style which is physical, content-centered, externally oriented, spatial, slow and concrete; 2) an attitude toward time present or past, rather than future-oriented; 3) resistance to change; 4) resignation to things as they are; and 5) dependence.[7]

Supporting the significance of social factors as causative factors of the mental set of developing societies, the second edition of the A.P.A. *Diagnostic and Statistical Manual of Mental Disorders* has included such diagnostic categories as social maladjustment "for individuals thrown into an unfamiliar culture ('culture shock') or into a conflict arising from divided loyalties to two cultures." The diagnostic category of occupational maladjustment can also be considered in this context.[8]

The problem of evaluating the traits of "the Latin American population according to the urban or rural residence from a psychological or psychiatric point of view," has been discussed by Adis in Costa Rica where he found a predominance of passive-aggressive and passive-dependent traits.[9]

The same problem is discussed by Carrizosa in Paraguay, who points out that a high number of neurotic and hysteric patients have not only recovered from their illness, but also that, after a periodic follow-up, some positive changes in their personalities had occurred. Carrizosa uses chemotherapy and a superficial psychotherapy with a high dose of suggestion. The success of the method is attributed to "the low cultural standard of the patients, the high degree of unsatisfied infantile needs, and the marked dependence on a paternalistic relationship."[10]

By fulfilling—consciously or not—some of the socially conditioned expectation of those patients, it was possible to achieve a definite improvement of symptoms that probably would resist techniques such as psychoanalysis, which are effective in other cultures.

A few psychological studies have evaluated the attitudes of Latin American people toward mental illness and psychiatric institutions. In Costa Rica, Adis found that a family may reject the patient when he returns from the hospital. On the other hand, the prevailing attitude toward the "mental asylum" is understanding, even though the term used in the study to refer to the mental hospital had a negative connotation.[11]

In Peru, Oetting and Stein observed the attitudes of the professional doctors and the auxiliary staff in four psychiatric hospitals. The cultural gap between these two levels of personnel is very wide. However, the existing communication problems do not seem to hinder the treatment of patients, since in both cultures their dignity is respected and the attitude of "blaming the patient" is avoided.

NOTES

1. U.N., *1967 Report on the World Social Situation,* p. 128.

2. Bowlby, J., *Maternal Care and Mental Health,* WHO Monograph Series, No. 2, Geneva, 1951.

3. Eisenberg, Leon, "Preventive Psychiatry, If Not Now, When?" *International Trends in Mental Health,* Henry P. David (Ed.), New York, McGraw-Hill, 1963, p. 63.

4. Ellul, J., *The Technological Society,* New York, Vintage Books, 1964, pp. 319–426.

5. Maury, M., *The Good War,* New York, Macfadden Books, 1965, pp. 134–40.

6. Chilman, C. S., *Growing Up Poor,* Washington, D.C., U.S. Department of Health, Education and Welfare, Welfare Administration Publication No. 13, 1966, p. 5.

7. Brotman, R. E., "Treatment of the Impoverished," in *Comprehensive Textbook of Psychiatry,* A. M. Freedman and H. I. Kaplan (Eds.), Baltimore, Williams and Wilkins, 1967.

8. American Psychiatric Association, *Diagnostic and Statistical Manual of Mental Disorders,* Second Edition, Washington, D.C., 1968.

9. Adis, Castro G., *Algunas Observaciones sobre la Investigacion en Psiquiatria Social,* Universidad de Costa Rica, 1968.

10. Carrizosa, A. *et al., Asistencia Psiquiatrica.*

11. Adis, Castro G., and Waisanen, F. R., "Lugar de Residencia y Actitude Hacia el Enfermo Mental," *Acta Psiquiatrica y Psicologica de America Latina,* 1965, Vol. 11, p. 356. Adis and Waisanen, "El Contexto Socioeconomico de las Actitudes Hacia el Enfermo Mental," *Acta Psiquiatrica y Psicologica de America Latina,* 1966, Vol. 12, p. 222. Adis and Waisanen, "El Caso de las Actitudes Hacia la Enfermedad Mental," *Acta Psiquiatrica y Psicologica de America Latina,* 1967, Vol. 13, p. 149.

12. Oetting, E. R., and Stein, W. W., "Popular Medical Beliefs and Attitudes Toward Mental Illness in Peru," *Human Organization,* 1966, pp. 308–11.

CHAPTER 8

Folk Psychiatry

CULTURAL PATTERNS AND PSYCHIATRY

IN reference to folk psychiatry, Kiev has written:

> Culture seems to influence the forms of illness and the kind of treatment developed to deal with them. It is for this reason that many of the treatment methods fit so neatly the needs of the patients with these disorders. That is to say, folk psychiatry can be defined as the culture-specific methods of anxiety reduction for the treatment of what appear to be culture-specific psychiatry disorders.[1]

If acquainted with folk psychiatry, doctors would enhance their efficiency by cooperating with and supervising witchdoctors, minimizing the contingent harmful effects of the latters' magical practices and using them as allies in the fight against physical and mental diseases within the population groups that are outside the usual scope of hospital care.[2] By understanding folk illnesses and therapies, Western-minded psychiatrists can more easily reach individuals of other cultures; psychiatry will also be better accepted if the public is not forced to abandon traditional beliefs.

As has been pointed out before (see Chapter 3), there are three groups in Latin America which, in spite of intimate contact with European culture during almost four centuries, retain a specific identity as non-Western cultures. Two of these groups are indigenous: the Indians who descend from high civilizations, and the primitive tribal Indians who never reached a state of complex civilization. The third group is the decendants of African people transplanted by the colonial slave trade.

Each group recognizes clear-cut folk illness syndromes and specific therapeutic methods. However, after such a long period of interaction among one another and with Latin European institutions, the present systems of thought and practice are manifestations of several cultural currents. The only exceptions are some primitive tribes that live in the forests of South America and who are almost unknown to white men.

The Folk Psychiatry of Hispanic American Indians

The inheritors of the Maya, Aztec, Inca, and other pre-Columbian civilizations have imprinted their culture from the southwestern states of the U.S.A. through Mexico and Central America, on Sapnish-speaking inhabitants as well as people who speak unrelated aboriginal languages such as Nahuatl in Mexico, Tzutzil in Guatemala, and Quechua in Peru. In spite of being a wide and variegated area, a common cultural complex of beliefs and attitudes is shared by all Spanish Americans.

There are, of course, local traits that distinguish the different groups from one another. Although most of these syndromes are heavily influenced by Spanish beliefs and Roman Catholicism, they are absent from historic or contemporary Spanish life.[3] That is to say, they are specific byproducts of syncretic Indian Hispanic culture, likely to be found wherever this culture is present. Two widespread folk illnesses are *susto* (fright), and *mal de ojo* (evil eye). *Susto* has been described in Texas by Kiev,[4] in Mexico and Guatemala by Rubel,[5] in Ecuador by Leon,[6] and in Peru by Chiape,[7] and we know of its occurrence in Bolivia and northern Argentina (*jujuy*). Although it is variously called *susto, espanto, jani,* or *pasmo,* the same folk etiology accounts for this illness: it is the loss of the soul, and the treatment is oriented to make the soul come back to its *asustado* (owner). The principal symptoms are restlessness, loss of appetite, weakness, and depression.

There are two explanations to account for soul loss. Among Spanish-speaking people a fright is thought to be the cause, and among Indian groups, *susto* is precipitated by an unintentional affront to the guardian spirits of the locality—divinities of the earth, water, animals—and the mischief must be expiated by propitiation of nature divinities before they will release the captured soul. It is necessary to sweep the body to remove the illness, using either an egg in Texas or a live guinea pig in Peru, and then the detached soul is called and guided to the body.

Susto undergoes a metamorphosis when the peasant migrates from his original community—such as *Ayllus* in Andean Heights—to modern cities. It not only changes its name to *dano* (in Peru), *maleficio* (in Colombia), or *envidia* (in San Antonio, Texas), but its etiology is also transformed and nature loses its predominance. The illness is now caused by the envy of wicked persons who pay sorcerers—*malero* in Peru, *brujas* in Mexico—to bewitch and cause harm to the victim. In this case, the specialist witchdoctor usually identifies the responsible person—a relative such as a mother-in-law, a boss, or a friend—with whom the patient has had difficulties, and after the performance of the curative rite, the victim is advised to avoid those troublesome relationships. Retaliation is never advised because it is accepted that evildoers are allied with powerful sorcerers.

The complex *dano–envidia–maleficio* replaces conflicts with nature with those of man against man which the urban migrant finds when he starts working for money instead of farming.

Without using supernatural concepts, Seguin[8] described in Lima a "Psychosomatic Syndrome of Maladjustment" in Indians who migrate from Peruvian highlands to coastal cities. After a latent period lasting from a week to a year, the patients show symptoms of anxiety, depression, and the most varied somatic signs; all symptoms disappear when doctors order the patients to return to their original villages and *Ayllus.*

The Mexican *curandero,* described by Kiev, and most of the Hispanic American witchdoctors, cure their patients by helping them to restore traditional ties. We can assume that Seguin's approach has been so effective because it also avoids the impersonal treatment offered by modern hospitals and doctors.

Mal de ojo, another widespread syndrome in Hispanic America, seems to have a parallel distribution to *susto.* Detailed descriptions have been written by Kiev in Texas[9] and Leon in Cali.[10] *Mal de ojo* (evil eye) affects children, causing an acute febrile illness with vomiting, diarrhea, and excessive crying. It strikes a child to whom affectionate overtures have been made; sometimes *mal de ojo* is caused unwittingly by a stranger who is not aware of the supernatural power of his gaze. In Cali, there are different gazes: some eyes have the power to dry (*ojo secador*) and cause dehydration in children or infertility in women; other eyes can cause fever, and so on. In Peru, there are white eyes and black eyes responsible for *mal de ojo.* A stranger who looked at the victim, or who smiled at a child, is the cause. After the diagnosis is made—for instance, by proving that the right foot is not the same length as the left—the witchdoctor prescribes a magic treatment which can involve the willing participation of the stranger responsible, thus proving that he did not intend any harm.

Localized syndromes have been widely reported. Such are the *empacho* and *caida de la mollera* of Mexican Americans.[11] The *flato* in El Salvador is a nervous tension caused by fear or sadness and characterized by insomnia and gastric complaints. The *tiricia* (for *ictericia = icterus*) is a Bolivian syndrome characterized by melancholia and crying. Folk syndromes in Peru include the *shucaque, tabardillo,* and *mal del aire,* the last of which is known as *hijillo* in El Salvador, and *hielo del difunto* in Colombia.[12]

In Costa Rica, Castro Adis[13] found that causes deriving from the supernatural and magic are becoming infrequent. Leon in Cali[14] reached a similar conclusion after finding that the contents of deliria and hallucinations have changed from the supernatural (demons, devils, souls) to another in which machines, apparatus, newspapers, or police predominate. The devil appears in Colombia, for instance, in a version adapted to contemporary realities, such as martians, astronauts, and communists, probably as a consequence of the so-called "revolution of awareness" brought about by the diffusion of the transistor radio, which surmounted the barriers of illiteracy and costly electrical installations. The ability to preserve certain traditions accounts for the survival of particular Indian health organizations such as the village of Salas in Peru and the *Kallawayas* from Bolivia, as well as for the persistent use of certain psychopharmacologically active substances.

In Salas, a village in the north of coastal Peru, folk medicine has become the principal source of income. It is a center for the treatment of *dano* and there are 200 *curanderos* living there out of a population of 1,500. People who are not directly involved in healing practices run "clinics" where patients and relatives coming from other zones are "hospitalized"; according to Chiape,[15] there is one "clinic" with 12 patients, and a patient told him that he had been hospitalized for six months in another "clinic." Clinics are poor dwellings with hotel-like services where diets are prepared with a prescription from the witchdoctor.

Witchdoctors in Salas claim to cure not only several folk syndromes, but also alcoholism. Also, they are able to detect illnesses beyond their powers to cure; patients are then usually referred to the city doctors. The most remarkable feature of any treatment in Salas is the use of *san pedro*, or *huachuma*, a beverage prepared by cooking the hallucinogenic cactus *Trichocereus Pachanoi* from which mescaline has been isolated.[16]

Witchdoctors, patients, and apprentices sniff the beverage during the healing ritual; then a "trip" similar to LSD intoxication helps the witchdoctor and the patient to see the person who caused the *dano* and to discover other cultural etiologies of the illness. The act of sniffing the beverage through the nose is called *singar*. Besides *san pedro*, witchdoctors use other beverages with tobacco, coca, alcohol, and *shimura*, or *cimora*, which according to Schultes[17] is an hallucinogenic drink derived from at least six plants, including *Trichocereus* and *Pachanoi*.

Kallawayas is the name of a Bolivian aboriginal group of itinerant medicine men who spend most of their time traveling through Indian America, from Chile to Mexico. *Kallawayas* use various plants to cure their patients. According to several botanists,[18] various seeds and herbs are used to form *vilca,* a juice poured into *chicha* (corn beer) and used as a laxative, emetic, aphrodisiac, and to dispel melancholia. *Vilca* probably contains seeds of *Anadenantera Columbina* and parts of plants from the genre *Virola* (*V. Sebifera*) from which psychoactive amines chemically related to bufotonine have been extracted.[19] The *Kallawayas* also use *malpighiaceas,* genre *Banisteriopsis* (*B. Caapi*), related to the vine *Ayahuasca* from northern Peru, which contains hallucinogenic substances and alkaloids of the harmala group—harmine and harmaline.[20]

But psychotropic drugs are not used merely for curative and divinatory reasons. The leaves of coca (*Erithroxicon Coca*), containing cocaine, are chewed by millions of Indians, constituting an endemic drug addiction which is now considered a serious public health problem and an enormous barrier to the social and economic development of the Andean Republics.

Besides the Andean psychotropic plants used by Indians, *peyote* in Mexico and Central America is famous as a hallucinogenic which has long been the center of religious and curative rites. Peyote is a small cactus (*Lophophora Williamsii*) that contains mescaline and other psychotropic substances. Mexican Indians also use narcotic mushrooms (genre *Psilocybe* and *Stropharia*) from which psilocybin has been isolated, and the seeds of *ipomea Violacea,* called *bado,* containing LSD-type alkaloids.[21]

FOLK PSYCHIATRY OF TRIBAL INDIANS

Primitive tribes inhabiting the lowlands surrounding the big South American rivers (the Amazon, the Orinoco, and the basin of the Rio La Plata) have been studied in Paraguay, Bolivia, Brazil, Peru, Ecuador, Colombia, Venezuela, and the Guayanas. Besides their anthropological and ethnopsychiatric interest, they are drawing attention from researchers looking for new psychotropic drugs known to most of these tribes. Among the members of such primitive cultures, treatment of disease usually comprises various kinds of exorcism, and diagnosis must be carried out through communication with the spirits of a supernatural world; many ways of communicating have been developed but the use of vision-producing narcotics or hallucinogens seems to be most widespread.

Hallucinogenic plants are not only used for diagnosis and treatment, but also when important ceremonies have to be conducted, such as the puberty rites of the Tucano Indians.[22] In some tribes hallucinogenic intoxications are used every day to stimulate exciting experiences, apparently without sacred or therapeutic motivation. This practice has been described among the Waikas, neighbors of the Tucano tribes.[23] Hallucinogenic snuffing powders are prepared with seeds and bark of leguminous plants such as *Anadenanthera Peregrina* (formely called *Piptatenia Peregrina*) and from the bark of *Virola Callophiloidea;* these plants have been chemically analyzed by Holmsted and Lindgren[24] who found many indole alkaloids in the specimens studied. The snuffs are known as *yopo, parica, epena,* and *cohoba.* Several of their components are not known, such as the components of the bark of the tree called *ama asita,* reported by Seitz.[25] During the intoxication, men communicate with the spirits (*Hekula*) and feel like giants (*macropsia*) flying above the earth.

The snuffing of plant materials for narcotic, especially for hallucinogenic, effects seems to be a peculiarly New World practice.[26] The habit is believed to have originated in the Amazonian and Sub-Andean region, probably with the Arawak Indians. Before the Spanish Conquest, and even before the Incas, this habit had spread to the highlands, presumably via the primitive inhabitants of northern Argentina (*jujuy*) and Chile (*Atacama*), where archeologists discovered tubes and trays artistically carved in wood and bone which were used as the paraphernalia of snuffing rites. Ethnographical and archeological researchers also have found snuffing paraphernalia in Tiahuanacu, the pre-Inca city near Titicaca Lake, between Peru and Bolivia, where snuffing of coca, tobacco, and other powder was associated with the cult of a divinity and human sacrifices. From South America the snuffing of narcotic and hallucinogenic powders spread to the Caribbean islands and Central America. At present, this habit has disappeared in the Andean and Caribbean regions, but Western culture is familiar with the snuffing of rappee and cocaine, both derived from South American plants: *N. Tabacum* and *E. Coca.*

We have already mentioned how the *curanderos* of Salas take hallucinogenic liquids through the nose. In northern Peru as well as in Amazonian Colombia and Ecuador, a drink for divination—usually swallowed, not snuffed—has been described under the complex *ayahuasca–caapi–yague–natem,* which contains the alkaloids harmine and harmaline, with I.M.A.O. (monoamine oxidase, monoamune oxidase inhibitory) action and hallucinogenic properties. Hallucinations with harmine are real perceptions of nonexistent objects, usually accompanied by physical sensations. On the other hand, intoxication with LSD and mescaline causes distortions of forms, movements, and colors from existing objects, and less frequent physical sensations.

Ayahuasca–Yaque–Caapi is prepared from vines from the headwaters of the Orinoco and Amazon rivers, principally of the species *Banisteriopsis–B. Caapi, B. Quitensis, B. Longialata, B. Metallicolor,* and related species: *Cabi paraensis, Lophantaera Lactecens,* and *L. Longifolia* from the *malpighiacea.* These plants have been studied by Deulofeau.[27] There are several reports from missionaries and explorers of another relatively unknown narcotic called *Marari,* used by Mojo Indians in Bolivia. *Marari* seems to be prepared from a plant related to *Verbenaceus.*[28]

THE FOLK PSYCHIATRY
OF AFRO AMERICANS

The slave trade spread African culture in the Circum-Caribbean area and coastal Brazil, where Africans formed a syncretism between African animism and Spanish, Portuguese, and French Catholicism and languages. We have described how the Inquisition in Cartagena and Mexico nipped in the bud the early syncretic cults in Colombia, Venezuela, and neighboring Puerto Rico and the Dominican Republic, but these cults grew up in Cuba as *santeria,*[29] in Haiti as *voodoo,*[30] and in coastal Brazil as *candombe.*[31] In the West Indies, the syncretic cult is known as *obeah.*

It should be noted that the followers of these Afro American cults participate in a distinctive subculture of the poor permeated with elements of African culture. Slavery was abolished in Cuba and Brazil less than 80 years ago.

Although these religions have been practiced secretly in the past, they currently enjoy relative freedom. In Brazil they form "nations" and in Haiti ceremonies take place under the approval of public officials; in Cuba, Catholic priests have always had a tolerant attitude toward African rites, as long as the ritualists were baptised.

In the Afro American religions a hierarchical structure of gods, saints, angels, and demons evolved into which Catholic saints, Christ, and the Virgin merge with African divinities and have a double name: one from the Roman Catholic Church and one from the African pantheon.[31a] These religions also involve a cult which includes a stratified clergy, temples, and propitiatory rites.

Bustamante[32] exhibited the etiological significance of *La Santeria* in a psychiatric disorder characterized by a sudden clouding of consciousness, which gives rise to a delirious and hallucinatory disturbance with bizarre or aggressive behavior. After having followed 200 of these patients over 20 years, Bustamante found that most of them shortly recovered completely. Owing to the sudden appearance and rapid recovery, these phenomena must be classified as a dissociative reaction or *Bouffee Delirante Aigue,* which seems to be far more frequent in Afro American cultures than among Western peoples. In Haiti, most of the abnormal but transitory states of trance and possession also are diagnosed as *Bouffee Delirante Aigue.*[33] This syndrome had sometimes been considered as acute schizophrenia, but after careful follow-up studies the latter diagnosis has been discarded.

Before the differential diagnosis was clear, most Western observers used to lump under the label of schizophrenic reactions, true acute or chronic schizophrenias with dissociations and trance states, as happened in a study carried out by Stainbrook in Brazil, where possession is very frequent in the *candomble* ceremonies.[34] Possession is the nucleus of cults and also of the folk etiology of psychiatric disorders in the Afro American population. During possession, the soul is replaced by another spirit. Then the possessed becomes the vehicle of the spirit, known as *loa* in Haiti.

Many possessed speak African dialects and perform extraordinary feats, such as climbing trees or walking barefoot over hot coals. After possession, amnesia is common.[35]

As Bastide has pointed out,[36] trance and possession among Africans are reached exclusively through music and dance. On the other hand, Latin American Indians induce trance through intoxication by psychotropic and hallucinogenic substances. Among Indians there is no concept of possession, or soul replacement, although the idea of soul loss or soul capture is the usual folk etiology of *susto*.

The relevance of the above mentioned illnesses and rites lies in their potential usefulness for the social psychiatrist who launches a program to reach people from another culture. As has been pointed out by Kiev:

> . . . it apepars that Haiti has a system of religious cult practices which serve both integrative and suppressive ends. The latter appear to be responsible in part for the difficulties encountered during attempts to introduce contemporary Western techniques of medicine in Haiti. . . . Voodoo exerts both therapeutic and anti-therapeutic effects. By cooperating with the voodoo priests, Western medicine can take advantage of the therapeutic potential inherent in voodoo practices and minimize the harmful effects of the *Hungan's* [voodoo priest] necessity to maintain prestige and power. He can be accorded the same prestige and influence but in a healthier as well as more medically sound way.[37]

It has also been found that an occult system of folk medicine —*obeah* in Trinidad—does cooperate with doctors and hospitals by taking care of psychiatric patients who are unable to get the attention they need from busy doctors and full hospitals.[38]

Reciprocally, a psychiatrist would find it easier to help African and Indian patients who consult him about rare problems if he is familiar with the socio-cultural background of these patients.

NOTES

1. Kiev, A., *Curanderismo, Mexican American Folk Psychiatry*, New York, The Free Press, 1968, p. 176.
2. Kiev, A. (Ed.), *Magic, Faith and Healing, Studies in Primitive Psychiatry Today*, New York, The Free Press, 1964.

3. Foster, G. M., "Relationships between Spanish and Spanish-American Medicine," *Journal of American Folklore,* 1953, Vol. 66, pp. 201–47.

4. Kiev, *Curanderismo.*

5. Rubel, A. J., "The Epidemiology of a Folk Illness: SUSTO in Hispanic America," *Ethnology,* 1964, Vol. 3, pp. 268–83.

6. Leon, C. A., "El Espanto, Sus Implicaciones Psiquiatricas," *Revista Colombiana de Psiquiatria,* 1966, Vol. I, p. 195.

7. Chiape, M., *Psiquiatria Folklorica Peruana, El Curanderismo en la Costa Norte del Peru,* Universidad de San Marcos, 1968 (mimeograph).

8. Sequin, C. A., "Migration and Psychosomatic Disadaptation," *Psychosomatic Medicine,* 1956, Vol. XIII, pp. 404–9.

9. Kiev, *Curanderismo.*

10. Leon, C. A., *El Mal de Ojo en Cali,* VII Congreso Colombiano de Psiquiatria, Cartagena, 1967 (mimeograph).

11. Kiev, *Curanderismo.*

12. Adis Castro, G., and Hernandez Urena, R., "Causas de Enfermedad Mental: Conceptos Populares," *Revista Interamericana de Psicologia,* 1967, Vol. I, pp. 297–312.

13. *Ibid.*

14. Leon, C. A., *El Diablo y el Almanaque,* V Congreso APAL, Bogotá, 1968 (mimeograph).

15. Chiape, *op. cit.*

16. Schultes, R. E., "The Place of Ethnobotany in the Ethnopharmacologic Search for Psychotomimetic Drugs," in Daniel H. Efron (Ed.), *Ethnopharmacologic Search for Psychoactive Drugs,* U.S. Dept. of Health, Education and Welfare, 1967. T. Pachonoi is a large cactus—1 to 10 feet in height—frequent in the Andean Highlands.

17. *Ibid.*

18. Siri von Reis Altshul, "Vilca and Its Use," in Daniel H. Efron (Ed.), *op. cit.*

19. Holmsted, Bo, and Lindgren, J. E., *Chemical Constituents and Pharmacology of South American Snuffs,* in Daniel H. Efron (Ed.), *op. cit.*

20. Claudio Naranjo, *Psychotropic Properties of the Harmala Alkaloids,* in Daniel H. Efron (Ed.), *op. cit.*

21. Naranjo, P., *Plantas Psicotropicas de America y Bioquimica de la Mente,* V Congreso APAL, Bogotá, 1968 (mimeograph).

22. Santa Cruz, A., "Un Ceremonial con Aspectos Psiquiatricos Transculturales entre ciertos Grupos Amerindios del Sudeste de Colombia," *Psiquiatria Transcultural,* La Habana, 1969, Vol. III, pp. 21–33.

23. Seitz, G. J., *Epena: the Intoxicating Snuff Powder of the Waika Indians and the Tucano Medicine Man, Agostino,* in Daniel H. Efron (Ed.), *op. cit.*

24. Holmsted and Lindgren, *loc. cit.*

25. Seitz, *loc. cit.*

26. Schultes, R. E., *The Botanical Origins of South American Snuffs,* in Daniel H. Efron (Ed.), *op. cit.*

27. Deulofeu, V., *Chemical Components Isolated from Banisteriopsis and Related Species,* in Daniel H. Efron (Ed.), *op. cit.*

28. Schultes, *loc. cit.*

29. Bustamante, J. A., "Factores Clinicos en Histerias con Cuadro

Clinico Esquizofrenico," *Psiquiatria Transcultural,* La Habana, 1968, Vol. II, pp. 10–16.

30. Kiev, A., "Spirit Possession in Haiti," *American Journal of Psychiatry,* 1961, Vol. 118, pp. 133–38; Douyon, E., "La Crisis de Posesion en el Vudu Haitiano," *Psiquiatria Transcultural,* La Habana, 1968, Vol. II, pp. 53–57.

31. Bastide, R., *Las Americas Negras,* Madrid, Alianza Editorial, 1969.

31a. Some equivalent names are: Jesus Christ = *Obatala* (in Brazil) = *Obatala* (in Cuba) = *Aizan* (in Haiti). The Holy Virgin = *Yemenja* = *Oshum* (both in Brazil). Saints Cosme and Damian = *Los Ibeyi* (Brazil) = *Los Jimaguas* (Cuba) = *Los Marassa* (Haiti). Source: Bastide, *op. cit.*

32. Bustamante, *loc. cit.* Bustamante, J. A., "El Bouffee Delirante en Nuestro Medio," *Psiquiatria Transcultural,* La Habana, 1969, Vol. 3, pp. 5–20.

33. Kiev, A., "Spirit Possession in Haiti," *American Journal of Psychiatry,* 1961, Vol. 118, pp. 133–38.

34. Stainbrook, E., "Some Characteristics of the Psychopathology of Schizophrenic Behaviour in Bahian Society," *American Journal of Psychiatry,* 1952, Vol. 109, pp. 330–35.

35. Kiev, "Spirit Possession . . ."

36. Bastide, *op. cit.,* p. 82.

37. Kiev, A., "Obstacles to Medical Progress in Haiti," *Human Organizations,* 1966, Vol. 25, pp. 10–15.

38. Borofsky, R., *Obeah. A Description of an Occult Medicine System in Trinidad,* Massachusetts, Brandeis University, 1968 (mimeograph).

PART TWO

Pilot Plan of Social Psychiatry (PPSP)

CHAPTER 9

The Nation
and the City

COLOMBIA

Geography

COLOMBIA, with an area of more than 1 million sq. km., is as large as Spain, France, and Portugal combined. It lies northwest of the South American subcontinent and is crossed from north to south by the Andes Mountains. Colombia is the only South American country with coasts on both the Atlantic and Pacific oceans. The environment ranges from equatorial rain forests to deserts, and temperature varies from tropical heat to perpetual snow. About 60 per cent of the total area of Colombia is east of the Andes, occupying the *llanos* of the Orinoco River and the forests of the Amazon. This vast region is almost unpopulated except for a few primitive nomadic tribes and some small isolated towns. Most of the active population and industrialized cities are located in the Andean region.

History

Before the Spanish Conquest, there seems to have been very little development of integrated societies in what is now Colombia. The Spaniards subdued the rival Indian tribes, of whom the *Chibchas* were the most prominent. Only in the southwest of the country, the population near Ecuador, which was part of the Inca empire, is the Indian influence significant.

New Granada, as the Spaniards called Colombia, followed much the same pattern as the other colonies of Latin America. The colonies were legally personal possessions of the Spanish king, and the majority of public posts were filled by Spaniards appointed by him. Trade was strictly regulated by Madrid.

The Catholic Church assumed a social and political role in New Granada which was to be of great importance in independent Colombia. Indeed, the "church question" has not been fully solved even now. The cultural expressions of Negroes in coastal Colombia were considered *bailes de brujas*,[1] or witches' dances, and those who participated in them were persecuted during the Inquisition. Negro culture is still present today in regional dances and family patterns.

Colombia gained political independence in 1819 as a part of the Republic of "Gran Colombia," comprising what is now Venezuela, Ecuador, and Colombia. This centralized republic was the culmination of Bolivar's campaign, but by 1830 and 1831 Gran Colombia was disrupted. After half a century of political chaos, Colombia attained some stability, and since 1836 it has been a democratic unitarian republic divided into 22 departments. At present, neither the Indian nor the Negro culture of Colombia is significant, so the population is fairly homogeneous in spite of racial heterogeneity.[2] Spanish traditions are predominant in the language, the loyalty to the Roman Catholic Church, the bullfights, and the paternalistic dual society in which the traditional landowner and the mercantile upper class hold many leading positions.

Population and Development

The present population of Colombia is almost 20 million. At an annual growth rate of 3.2 per cent, this figure will double in 22 years. The rural rate of growth is 1.9 per cent, but the urban rate is 7.2. No less than 42.6 per cent of the population is younger than 14 years of age, and more than 60 per cent live in rural areas. Life expectancy at birth was calculated in 1964 at 60 years. The gross domestic annual income per capita was $268 (U.S.) in 1965.[3] Colombia's economy has long been excessively dependent on coffee exportation, but this monocultural dependence has been relieved to some extent by the emergence of industrial centers such as Cali and Medellin, and by the production of cotton and sugar since 1960. Nevertheless, production is insufficient and development limited. With coffee especially, production is limited by the underpoduction on *minifundios,* or small holdings, which are not economically viable. Land tenure systems that are almost feudal hold back productivity and make it extremely difficult to bring the workers in such areas above the mere subsistence level. In rural zones, the illiteracy rate is twice that of the cities, and 80 per cent of housing is in bad condition. The National Institute of Land Reform (INCORA) is currently attempting to solve these problems.

In Colombia, economic and social development is heterogeneous. The economy is suffering from recurring cycles of inflation which increase unemployment and the cost of living. As for occupation, 54 per cent of the population depends on agriculture and only 12 per cent on industry. The rest is engaged in public and domestic services, petty trade or unspecified activities.

As in other Latin American countries, the most conspicuous phenomenon of today's Colombia is rapid urban growth, based primarily on rural migration, and second on swift natural growth. In the bigger cities, districts of "clandestine" houses—built without permit—have grown up around the urban centers.[4]

These clandestine houses have the usual disadvantages of no electricity, running water, or sanitation,[5] and are sometimes built on land unsuitable for development—in Cali, for example, on steep slopes severely affected by erosion. The housing shortage is even worse in the countryside. Nevertheless, Columbia is—with Chile and Costa Rica—one of the three Latin American countries that have been able to raise their level of housing production to somewhat above 3 units per 1,000 people during the 1960's. It has done so by stressing minimum housing costs under the direction of the Territorial Credit Institute (ICT). Urbanization has been accompanied by poor and crowded living conditions, underemployment, and family disintegration, which is reflected in the high rate of illegitimate births.

These problems are compounded by the high illiteracy rate—which includes over 30 per cent of those over 15 years—and by social problems such as alcoholism and crime. Crime and alcoholism are usually associated. In 1964, 21 per cent of the people indicted for crime were under the effects of alcohol.

"La Violencia" (Violence)

La Violencia, or large-scale bandit and guerrilla activity, prominent in rural areas, has been a problem in Colombia. *La Violencia* started in 1949 and lasted more than 15 years. It was characterized by bizarre mass killings and sexual offenses which caused the deaths of at least 200,000 people and forced many peasants to leave their villages for urban centers. It is assumed that *la Violencia* had its roots in the country's traditional agrarian structure. Leon[6] has presented a psychoanalytically oriented paper showing how some of the peasants' patterns of child rearing might account for the sadistic crimes of *la Violencia.*

Health Resources[7]

Doctors are the most numerous health personnel in the country, with 1 for every 2,300 persons. Latin America averages 1 doctor per 1,700 people; the United States, 1 per 700. The rate of nurses at the university level is 1 per 16,000 inhabitants. In South America as a whole the rate is 1 nurse per 4,000, and in the United States, 1 per 314. There are 3,500 certified assistant nurses. The number of laboratory technicians, sanitary engineers, nutritionists, and other specialists is lower. Furthermore, the number of young people interested in following nursing courses at the university is extremely low.

Presently, medical schools can handle 995 graduates a year, but this potential is hindered by a dropout rate of 30 per cent.

The geographical distribution of doctors shows that 74 per cent are concentrated in the main urban areas, where only 31 per cent of the population lives. In big cities, the average rate is 1 doctor per 1,000 inhabitants, whereas in the rest of the country the rate is 1 per 6,300. Doctors engaged in private and non-private practice simultaneously include 65 per cent; 15 per cent are engaged solely in private practice, and almost 30 per cent have followed specialized training programs. Most professional nurses practice in public institutions; only 14 per cent work in private clinics. The concentration of active nurses in main urban areas is 86 per cent.

The percentage of national government expenditures for health in 1965 was 4.7, but there is no proportionate distribution of public expenses on health matters, since certain groups of insured individuals absorb 43 per cent of these expenses, even though they represent hardly 10 per cent of the population. The remaining 90 per cent accounts for only 57 per cent of the expenses.

Hospital beds are available at the rate of 2.7 per 1,000 inhabitants, with an unequal distribution between the various departments. Although in Bogotá there are 4.5 hospital beds per 1,000 persons, on the Atlantic coast there are only 1.4. One of every three hospital beds remains unoccupied, while the average period of hospitalization is high—11.2 days—which shows that beds are underutilized.

The poor rural population benefits less from health resources, although it needs them more urgently and frequently. In brief, it can be concluded that the medical staff of the country is being inadequately utilized. The availability of doctors and nurses is threatened by the increasing emigration rate; the required nursing care cannot be provided by the staff available, nor by the one that could be trained under the present system. Better use of the human resources available requires paramedical and auxiliary personnel, proper equipment for rendering services, and improvement in working and educational conditions. The training of doctors and nurses must be carried out according to the conditions and actual needs of the country, and must enable them to keep pace with new scientific discoveries.

Mental Health[8]

Presently, there are 7,500 beds for psychiatric patients in 27 institutions, and there are 7,800 hospitalized patients. Psychiatric institutions throughout the country are heterogeneous regarding the medical care provided.

Mental disorders, measured by the number of visits to doctors, accounted for 1,762.2 visits per 100,000 persons in 1967. In 1965, the average number of days of hospitalization per mental patient was 115. There are 162 psychiatrists in Colombia, and, while there is an obvious lack of integration of medical services in the country as a whole, this is even more evident in the field of psychiatry. The psychiatrists themselves lack unity in their diagnostic and therapeutic criteria. Psychiatric services are not divided by geographical areas. Eleven departments have no mental care services whatsoever, and out of 646 general hospitals, only 6 provide psychiatric services. There are 5 nurses specialized in psychiatry, and 83 working in this field without specialization. The number of psychiatric aides is estimated at 250. For the present population of Colombia, 1,000 psychiatrists, 2,000 psychologists, and 4,000 social workers would be needed in order to have an ideal team of 1 psychiatrist, 2 psychologists, and 4 social workers per 20,000 inhabitants. Presently, there is only 1 psychiatrist per 120,000 persons, and but 1 medical psychologist per 280,000 inhabitants. Even worse, 64 per cent of the psychiatrists and psychologists work in Bogotá, and most of them are engaged in private practice.

The psychiatric problem in Colombia may be partially evaluated on the basis of the following information: It is estimated that 13 out of every 1,000 people suffer from neurosis, and 5 out of every 1,000 from psychosis. Of every 1,000 persons, 8 have deficiencies, 6 are alcoholics, and 9.5 are epileptics. Epilepsy is more common in rural areas. The suicide rate is 6.1 per 100,000 inhabitants.[9]

Homicide reached a rate of 48.1 per 100,000 in 1958, the

highest in the Americas, exacerbated by *la Violencia,* although this rate is decreasing. The consumption of alcohol was 1.97 liters per capita in 1965. Prostitution and delinquency are growing.

There is a national mental health plan, operative through 1977, which represents the greatest effort yet to provide mental health programs for the Colombian society.

In various studies and recommendations, the need to train auxiliary personnel, including "psychiatric technicians," and to develop external preventive work is stressed. Epidemiological and psycho-social research, integration and better coordination of services and, in general, the development of a true social psychiatry of the community are also emphasized.

Modern medicine is available only to the wealthiest urbanites, a small fraction of the population. In 1962, out of 836 cities of Colombia, 665 had no doctor, and only 10 cities had psychiatrists. In rural areas primitive healers fulfill some of the therapeutic and social functions of physicians. Some of these healers, such as the *curioso* from the banks of the Magdalena River, specialize in mental disorders.[10]

Presently, there is also a boom in popular medical practices performed by self-styled psychologists, mentalists, spiritualists, astrologists, chiromancers, and hypnologists, who abound in every city of Colombia. They are limited by the law of medical practice. Moreover, the Society of Psychiatry has launched several campaigns to warn the public against the consequences of the so-called occult sciences.[11] Even if these practices were harmless, they still compete with scientific medicine and hinder the progress of public health. Furthermore, they bar epidemiological research, particularly in the field of mental health, because of their secrecy.

Nevertheless, these activities profit because they satisfy emotional needs in the depersonalized and fragmented environment of poor marginal zones, possibly because they are as traditionally oriented as the mind of the general population.

Cali

This city is the capital of the Department Valle del Cauca, or Valle. Santiago de Cali was founded in 1536 by Sebastian Benalcazar, one of Pizarro's captains, who conquered the Cauca Valley. The history of this city goes back more than four centuries, yet the processes of industrialization and economic development began only after World War II.

With about 1 million inhabitants, Cali is considered the third city in Colombia. Bogotá, the capital, is the largest and most populated, and Medellin is the most important center of industry and business. Cali shares with these two cities, and also with Barranquilla in the north, the characteristics and changes of rapid urbanization and economic development. Geographically, it is located in the Cauca Valley between two branches of the Andes. This is a tropical zone with land especially fertile for the cultivation of sugar cane. Cali is separated from the Pacific Ocean only by one of the branches of the Andes. The important Pacific port of Buenaventura is linked to Cali by a railroad.

As the most important city in southwest Colombia, Cali attracts massive migration from smaller cities and rural areas. This plus a high fertility rate account for the very high rate of population growth—over 6 per cent a year. In spite of having a progressive industry, unemployement is a problem. The prosperous commercial center seems disproportionately tiny in the midst of the ever-growing marginal shanty towns. The city reflects on the one hand the energy of its industrial progress, with skyscrapers and elegant residential sectors, and on the other, a lack of urban planning reflected in the chaotic surroundings, or *barrios populares*. The ICT is working to abate the housing problem. Rapid and hitherto uncontrolled urban growth has led to high rates of crime and juvenile delinquency, often associated with alcoholism and disintegrated families.

Inadequate educational and social services are reflected in high rates of illiteracy, malnutrition, and infectious diseases. The Universidad del Valle is the principal institution for training technical personnel and controlling problems of public health, as well as other social problems in Cali and smaller towns in the area.

The medical school of the Universidad del Valle is similar to the American model. It consists of several departments which train medical students and postgraduate doctors who begin their specialization after internship and residency, including a number of foreigners who will return to their native countries elsewhere in Latin America.

The Department of Psychiatry of the Facultad de Medicina de Universidad del Valle

The "Plan Piloto de Psiquiatria Social" (Pilot Plan of Social Psychiatry, PPSP) was launched in 1967. Before describing the PPSP, however, a schematic presentation of the activities that are accomplished in the Department of Psychiatry will be given as a background to explain the plan.[12]

When the PPSP was instituted, the Department of Psychiatry had a staff of 10 psychiatrists (four of whom were working full time in the department), one clinical psychologist, and three social workers. This staff was engaged in a number of activities which could be roughly classified as educational, therapeutic, and research. These activities were carried on in the medical school, the Hospital Universitario del Valle, which is a general hospital with 500 beds, and the Hospital Psiquiatrica San Isidro (HPSI). Among the educational activities, the most important were teaching psychiatry to medical students[12a] and training residents. The students receive 50 hours of psychobiology during the third year; 90 hours of psychopathology during the fourth year, and 110 hours of clinical psychiatry in the fifth. All these courses are divided into theoretical lectures, discussion groups, and practical seminars with patients.

During the sixth year, students—the clerks—rotate through the psychiatric hospital in groups of four or five during a period of four weeks. They participate in the treatment of in-patients and learn to take adequate clinical histories. They also rotate through the service of psychosomatic medicine, accumulating a total of 230 hours of psychiatric work.

The intern, or seventh-year student, rotates through the psychiatric hospital for one month. He works in the out-patient department and also with hospitalized patients; he is in charge of emergencies during nights and weekends and also participates in seminars on psychosomatic medicine. He passes a total of 230 hours of work in psychiatry. The post-graduate residency lasts three years. The first-year resident works in the wards of the psychiatric hospital and in the out-patient department. He also attends a number of seminars which train him in the treatment of patients using both physical and psychological techniques, and give him a review of the basic sciences in relation to psychiatry.

The second-year resident provides psychiatric consultation and treatment to the students of the Universidad del Valle and receives intensive training in psychodynamics and phychotherapy. He also takes care of special patients in the psychiatric hospital.

The third-year resident, while continuing the same activities as the other residents, also receives training in child psychiatry, supervises the work of interns and medical students in psychosomatic medicine, and is in charge of the Pilot Plan of Social Psychiatry.

During the three years of residency, the trainee is closely supervised by the members of the staff.

The HPSI used to be an asylum for chronic patients who received only custodial care in conditions of misery and filth, until, in 1955, the university included this hospital in the medical school. The HPSI is now an institution with modern buildings and gardens which occupies an area of about 40,000 square miles, and is only 10 miles away from the commercial center of Cali. The HPSI has facilities for 300 hospitalized patients,[12b] an out-patient department, occupational therapy, day-hospital, medical, neurological, and dental services, and a social work unit. It also has facilities for housing interns and residents. HPSI has fifteen registered nurses and about 100 aides. It is basically oriented toward short and intensive treatment of acute cases. Nevertheless, it has almost 100 beds for the long-term treatment of chronic patients. Those patients who need continued treatment are usually handled through the out-patient department, where they receive medicines and psychotherapy. If a family prefers a longer hospitalization for a patient, they are referred to the psychiatric hospital in Pasto, a city in the south of Colombia. In general, very few patients—three to five a year—need to be referred to Pasto.

Psychiatric research activities include the study of new drugs, especially those with anti-depressive and anti-psychotic effects, and studies of transcultural psychiatry (which have been mentioned elsewhere in this work).[13]

The epidemiological and social aspects of psychiatry are researched in the Department of Psychiatry; problems of urbanization and public health in their widest context, such as marital stability, nutrition, delinquency, abortion, and suicide also are studied. These studies aim at elucidating the natural history of psychiatric illnesses and their demographies. This research had major significance for the systematic planning of the PPSP, helping to assess local conditions and to take into account local attitudes and local needs before starting activities in the field.[14]

NOTES

1. Roselli, H., "La Inquisicion en Cartagena de Indias," in *Historia de la Psiquiatria Colombiana,* Bogotá, Horizontes, 1968.

2. Ethnic distribution in percentage of the total Colombian population: Mixed 65, White 25, Negro 5, Indian and others, 5.

3. These figures have their source in the U.N. publication *1967 World Social Situation,* pp. 126–27.

4. Lyonette, K. J., *Colombia,* in Claudio Veliz (Ed.), *Latin America and the Caribbean, A Handbook.*

5. Sociedad Colombiana de Psiquiatria, *Informe Sobre La Salud Mental En Colombia,* 1968 (mimeograph). Fifty-five per cent of the houses have no running water; 45 per cent lack toilet facilities; 40 per cent consist only of a single room or hut; and 20 per cent are used by more than one family.

6. Leon, C. A., *Unusual Patterns of Crime During "La Violencia" en Colombia,* 124th Annual Meeting, American Psychiatric Association, Boston, 1968 (mimeograph).

7. Sociedad Colombiana de Psiquiatria, *op. cit.*

8. *Ibid.* For a wider approach, see also Kiev, A., *La Psiquiatria Social en Colombia,* V Congreso APAL, Bogotá, 1968.

9. Rendon, *op. cit.* In the cities, suicide rates are higher—around 18 per 1,000 inhabitants in Cali and 12 in Bogotá.

10. Roselli, H., "Aspectos de la Medicina Indigena y la Psiquiatria Popular," in *Historia de la Psiquiatria Colombiana,* Bogotá, Horizontes, 1968.

11. Roselli, H., "Indagaciones en el Misterio—Cronologia del Hipnotismo," in *Historia de la Psiquiatria Colombiana,* Bogotá, Horizontes, 1968.

12. Perdomo, R., *Estado Actual de la Docencia e Investigacion en Psiquiatria en el Area de Cali y Popayan,* VII Congreso Colombiano de Psiquiatria, Cartagena, 1967 (mimeograph).

12a. In Cali, as in most Latin American universities, the teaching of medicine consists of seven years. The sixth year is dedicated to the supervision of practical activities of students who rotate through different services. The seventh year is the same as the American internship.

12b. Only 220 beds are used by the university. The remaining 80 beds are used for the Colombian Institute of Social Security and for private patients.

13. Perdomo, R., "Estado Actual de la Docencia e Investigacion en Psiquiatria en el area de Cali y Popayan," VII Congreso Nacional de Psiquiatria, Cartagena, 1967 (mimeograph).

14. *Plan Piloto de Psiquiatria Social,* Cali, Departamento de Psiquiatria, Facultad de Medicina, Universidad del Valle, 1967. Kiev, A., "Activities of the International Committee Against Mental Illness," *Transcultural Psychiatric Research,* Montreal, 1969, Vol. 6, pp. 89–92.

CHAPTER 10

PPSP: Rationale and Locale

CLARIFICATION OF OBJECTIVES

THE PPSP was intended to demonstrate the type of comprehensive psychiatric services which can be introduced among Latin American marginal populations. Second, as a social psychiatry plan, it was directed toward ". . . the study of social factors contributing to the onset, course and outcome of mental illness and the adequate organization of community care."[1] Within this broad area, a number of sub-goals warrant additional description.

In the model or pilot for demonstration, changes are initiated on a small scale, and meticulous observations are made of the process. These observations are carried on in the community where the PPSP operates, emphasizing the study of psychiatric patients and their families. Furthermore, the agents of change—psychiatrists and allied personnel—being part of the project, are also undergoing change, and they themselves must be observed. The careful report and analysis of the observations—which presuppose accurate recording and filing of the information—will eventually lead to a knowledge of what is being done, of how to prevent unnecessary repetition or backward steps, and of how to compare the results with other projects and to help initiate new programs with more confidence, precision, and speed. A circular feedback—both in time and space—will facilitate the aims and activities of social psychiatry.

The fundamental aim of any activity in psychiatry has certainly to be the ". . . attainment by all peoples of the highest possible level of mental health." In 1951, WHO's Expert Committee on Mental Health stated that ". . . mental health . . . implies the capacity of the individual to form harmonious relations with others, and to participate in, or contribute constructively to, changes in his social and physical environment. It implies also his ability to achieve a harmonious and balanced satisfaction of his own potentially conflictive instinctive drives."[2]

However, ". . . the appraisal of mental health must be dependent on a value system which is inherent in the community from which the individual is drawn."[3]

Margaret Mead says that:

> The psychiatrists working in the industrialized West may come to emphasize the hazards of the weakened family structure and the broken home. But the psychiatrists working in unindustrialized sections of the world may simultaneously be emphasizing the hazards of a too closely knit family for the mental health of individuals who, later in life, must adapt to the impersonal system of human relations which will come with the introduction of modern industry.[4]

This statement points out the necessity of starting psychiatric work on the local level in order to develop the concepts which are compatible with each situation or locale. The most practical step is to ensure that as psychiatric practice grows in countries where it is as yet undeveloped, the psychiatrists have every opportunity to work closely with social scientists.

The rationale of the PPSP—besides its serving as a model—is

briefly as follows. There is an enormous burden of disability associated with mental illness, and the tools and knowledge available to ameliorate this disability are undermined by traditional approaches to the problem of mental health in the attitudes of both the public and psychiatrists. Consequently, the PPSP was designed to provide extra-mural training for psychiatrists as a period of practice and experience attached to a field research unit (or pilot plan) with opportunities to become familiar with the principles and methods of epidemiology and such social sciences as social psychology and social anthropology. The field, or extra-mural, training will help also to assess the needs and resources of a community in terms of preventive psychiatry. The prevention of psychiatric disorders can be met at three levels:

Knowledge at the *primary prevention* level is scarce and new. However, it is aimed at promoting mental health and providing specific protection from situations which are known to contribute to an increase in mental disorders (crises, accidents, chronic diseases, etc.). The promotion of mental health could be attained through pre-matrimonial, pre-natal, family, and school counseling and improved housing, working conditions, education, nutrition, and public health.

Secondary prevention aims at the early diagnosis, treatment, and recovery of those who are already ill.

Tertiary prevetion helps to rehabilitate and to avoid further deterioration of some patients who cannot be completely cured, but who cannot be considered hopeless.

This broad conception of preventive psychiatry[1] is summed up by Ari Querido: "Public health approach to mental disorders is the same as with other illnesses: prevent what we know how to prevent; terminate and mitigate what we know how to terminate and mitigate; reduce disabilities resulting from illness."[5]

A special strategy had to be developed to meet the demands of a project of social psychiatry and to maximize the potential resources to be found in the community in a poor marginal group, such as Cali.

The strategy of the PPSP was divided into four areas:
1) The study and utilization of existing facilities;

2) The education and training of available manpower;

3) The organization of teamwork and integration of services and functions;

4) Research.

These activities will be dealt with in forthcoming pages, when it will be easier to evaluate the PPSP, and to five further recommendations.

DESCRIPTION
OF THE FACILITIES

The PPSP was to use the facilities of medical centers which already offered public health services, but no psychiatric care, to the community. There are several advantages to such an arrangement. This was a way of facilitating the integration of mental and public health; these centers already had the necessary physical installations; medical and personal contacts were already established with the people; an expert staff was available to care for the physical problems of the community, and, finally, the same facility could be used to provide practical training for the medical personnel. The combination of these advantages meant crucial savings in time and expense and the utilization of prestigious and well-developed medical centers as pre-conditions for new programs served to pave the way for planned innovations.

It happened that one of the three medical centers selected for the PPSP, the Luis H. Garces Center in Cali's *barrio* Villanueva, had begun its activities recently and its staff was in the stage of organizing medical activities. After a few months of psychiatric work, it was found that problems in other areas prevented the center's staff from participating in the plan. On the other hand, in the other two centers, the activities of the PPSP were accepted without noticeable resistance. These two centers are today the location of the PPSP, with an increasing range of activities and a number of operations in the field.

To simplify the description of the PPSP, the activities of each of these two centers—El Guabal and Candelaria—will be reported separately. But it should be borne in mind that they are parts of a single project.

EL GUABAL

El Guabal is one of the typical *barrios populares* (popular districts) that surround Cali. It was founded in southern Cali in 1960 as one of the projects of the ICT (Instituto de Credito Territorial) to provide low-cost housing. Before its urbanization it was a farm which was frequently flooded by the Cali River. Because of the distribution of lots by the ICT, El Guabal does not have the chaotic disorganization of older slums in the eroded slopes near Cali. However, the streets are unpaved, the houses have insufficient water supplies, and only a few have modern toilet facilities.

In 1967, the estimated population approached 15,000. This population represents a structure typical of the rapid urbanization and growth characteristic of Colombia and Latin America. From a survey of 520 families in 1968, it was found that 90.26 per cent of the population was under 45 years of age, 70 per cent was under 25, and 52.5 per cent was under 15.

Although the children of El Guabal receive some health care from the Medical Center—which has been especially successful in the prevention of infectious diseases—they still suffer social and psychological deprivations which render them unable to adapt to school, and later on to work and society.

Thanks to the Medical Center, mortality rates are low, but fertility is still very high. There are energetic programs to spread concepts of planned parenthood throughout the community and to make the new contraceptive methods acceptable to the people. It can be said for El Guabal that "Our number one problem is population," as a Colombian minister told the Rockefeller mission,[6] but birth control is still an emotional and controversial issue. A psychiatric program could help deal with the anxieties and fears aroused by individual and family discussions of this topic. The birth control programs in El Guabal have so far succeeded in reducing the birth rate from 35.6 per 1,000 people a year in 1962 to 18.7 in 1966.

But El Guabal is still growing at an annual rate of 60.3 persons per 1,000, mainly because of the immigration of people from other *barrios* in Cali, from rural areas near the city, and from distant areas in other *departamentos* where industrialization has not yet begun. Almost the entire adult population of El Guabal was born outside Cali. The population has a high rate of mobility—26.43 per cent of the families in a survey of 250 families in 1968 had been living in the barrio for less than three years, and the average length of residency for these 520 families was 5.3 years. In the same survey, it was found that the average number of persons in each family was 7.2, defining as one family the group of individuals who share housing and food. The average per capita income was around $112 (U.S.) a year in that survey. (The average for Colombia is $268 [U.S.] per capita.) Although very few people have completed the five compulsory years of primary education, the illiteracy rate is remarkably low—only 1.8 per cent of the population older than 15. (The estimates for Colombia give a rate of illiteracy of 30.5 per cent.) However, we do not have data about "functional illiterates"; i.e., adults with less than four years of school.

In 1966, the rate of deaths per 1,000 was 3.5. In Colombia as a whole, the rate is 9.9 per 1,000. Proportions of male and female adults are almost the same among the population of El Guabal, which would indicate that most of the people, especially young migrants, live with their families. The proportions of single and married people are equivalent in the adult population (in the medical department of El Guabal, an adult is an individual older than 15). Only 3.8 per cent of this group live as common law partners, which is a rate lower than in the rest of Colombia.

Widows account for 1.52 per cent of a sample of 3,774 persons, and divorced or separated persons for 1.19 per cent. Racially, El Guabal does not differ from the rest of Colombia. Mestizos (or "mixed") predominate, and there are small proportions of whites, Negroes, and Indians. More than 90 per cent are Roman Catholic.

There is some overcrowding in El Guabal because some of the owners rent one or more rooms to another family to have an additional, though modest, source of income. This situation is compounded by the fact that families usually have numerous children. In 1966 the total number of housing units was 1,865, while the number of families was 2,300.

SAN JUAN BAUTISTA, THE PAROCHIAL CENTER

When ICT started the construction of El Guabal, the private foundation *Hernando Carvajal* built the *Centro Parroquial San Juan Bautista* (St. John the Baptist Parochial Center), which provides the people a comprehensive program of social and medical services. This center is divided into six departments:

1) Religion, with a church and priest;

2) Education, with a primary school;

3) Physical education and sports, with game grounds for soccer, basketball, etc.;

4) Discount store, which sells high-protein food and medicines at low prices, as well as many other articles;

5) Welfare, run by social workers;

6) Medical, run by the Department of Preventive Medicine of the School of Medicine, Universidad del Valle, offering complete public health services. It also has a community promotion program offering courses in cooking, sewing, gardening, and poultry and rabbit breeding as sources of income and protein.

Since July 1967 the PPSP has been merged with the Medical Department to use the existing facilities and personnel serving the community. The psychiatrist in charge was supposed to organize his activities without interfering with the functions of the former program and without demanding excessive work from the already busy staff.

Psychiatric patients and medical patients had to share the waiting room, offices, and clinical histories as well as doctors and allied health personnel. In this way one of the objectives of the PPSP—to integrate mental health into a public health service program—was fulfilled. The immediate gain from such integration was that the PPSP started to function within a community which was accustomed to accepting innovations in the field of health as desirable. In addition, periodic surveys yielded accurate data and a useful rapport had been established with the local population.

In December 1966 the Medical Department had records of 1,805 families, 75.2 per cent of the 2,400 families estimated to live in El Guabal. This is good coverage, especially considering the short time the center has been in existence and the difficulties which had to be overcome to reach these people. In theory, the Medical Department provides care to 12,600 persons (1,805 families with 7 persons each).

The therapeutic unit for the medical department in El Guabal is not the individual but the dwelling unit, so it happens that each clinical history contains the information of one complete family, and in some cases of two families—the owner's and the tenant's. Under this system, each history can be located on the map of the *barrio,* because the histories have the same numerals as the houses.

El Guabal is divided into three zones:

Zone I. Originally called the zone *of unfinished houses,* it is now known as *Barrio Panamericano,* revealing the inhabitants' wish not to be identified with a poor *barrio.* Here the ICT gave each family a lot and an unfinished house which had to be decorated by the occupants. The monthly payment for these houses is around $10 (U.S.). The dwellings look pleasant and comfortable. Inside there is usually a television set and a refrigerator as symbols of status, and most of the houses have modern furniture, kitchens, and sanitary services connected to public sewers. In 1966, 605 housing units (32.4 per cent of the total in El Guabal) were located in Zone I.

People in this zone cooperate very well with the programs of the parochial center, and accept the PPSP with no difficulty. They account for 34.3 per cent (619 families) of the families registered with the medical department in 1966.

Zone II. Called the zone of mutual assistance, this is the largest and central zone of El Guabal. It surrounds the parochial center and consequently benefits most from the medical department. Zone II had 756 houses in 1966 (40.5 per cent of the total) and accounted for 731 (40.5 per cent) of the families registered in the files of the medical department.

Here the families receive land and construction materials from the ICT to build their houses. The monthly installments to be paid to the ICT are from about $4–6 (U.S.).

Zone III. Called the zone of personal effort, this is the poorest zone in El Guabal. ICT provides only the land, and the people build their own houses with cheap materials such as bamboo. The standards of living here are of mere subsistence and dire poverty. The monthly payments to the ICT range from $1–2 (U.S.), In 1966 this area was the least populated—there were only 504 houses (27.1 per cent of the total). Moreover, it receives fewer services from the parochial center than the other zones. Only 455 families (25.2 per cent) from this zone are registered in the medical department files.

This is why El Guabal, in spite of being a marginal and lower-class *barrio,* cannot be considered of uniform population. Instead, it is divided into three socio-economic strata, the highest of which corresponds to Zone I, and the lowest to Zone III.

CANDELARIA

This municipality was founded in 1545. Four centuries have not changed a way of life which originated in the Middle Ages. Only during the last two decades have technology and the reforms of the land tenure system helped to rapidly develop the social and economic conditions of its people.

Candelaria covers 286 sq. km. It is located in the south of the Departamento del Valle, sharing boundaries at the south with the Departamento de Cauca and at the north with the municipality of Cali.

In 1968 the estimated population was 31,570, scattered in small nuclei of less than 6,000 people. According to a survey of a sample of 210 families, 48.5 per cent of the population is under 15 and 91.4 per cent is under 45. The population growth is determined both by high fertility and the constant migration from other departments, especially from Narino, at the boundary with Ecuador. The population grows at a rate of 6.5 per cent annually.

The whole region is rural, and the principal occupation is the cultivation of sugar cane.

As in other areas of Colombia, the race which predominates is Mestizo, followed by Negro, white, and Indian populations, and the religion is Roman Catholic.

The average number of persons per family is 6.9. The general mortality rate was 9.4 per 1,000 people in 1968. Infant mortality diminished from 137 per 1,000 in 1963 to 99.1 per 1,000 in 1968.

Two different socio-economic surveys, one in 1966 and the other in 1969, revealed that the average income per capita is about $90 (U.S.) annually. It is estimated that 25 per cent of the population older than 15 years is illiterate, but there are numerous schools and residents are highly motivated to improve their education. Sixty-eight per cent had less than 3 years of schooling. The male population is larger than the female, especially in the 25- to 35-year-old age group. This predominance could be explained by the men's habit of migrating and working away from home. Half the adult men work as day laborers in the sugar cane fields.

The high geographical mobility is shown in the results of the survey of 210 families in 1969: 23 per cent had been living less than five years in Candelaria, and only 8 per cent had been born there. In the main nucleus of the population, 20 per cent of the families live in hired dwellings and pay an average sum of $8 (U.S.) a month for rent. Of the houses, 61 per cent are considered inadequate and non-hygienic.

The land tenure system resembles the general situation in Colombia: 87 per cent of the land is held by 11 per cent of the owners, while the rest of the population holds the remaining 13 per cent.

Since July 1958 the Universidad del Valle has been responsible for the public health activities of the municipality of Candelaria. The university created a health center with 22 beds for training the medical and allied personnel in education, medical care, and research activities. Now Candelaria is the rural laboratory of the School of Medicine. It has facilities which allow the realization of different projects at minimal cost. The community is periodically surveyed by questionnaires and interviews and, in general, innovations in health activities are welcomed.

The expenses of this health center are 1,319,606 Colombian pesos (about $80,000 [U.S.]), 36.6 per cent of which are dedicated to research and teaching. Of this amount, 3.7 per cent goes to the PPSP.

NOTES

1. WHO, *Technical Report Series,* No. 252, p. 25.
2. *Ibid.,* No. 223, p. 13.
3. *Ibid.*
4. Mead (Ed.), *op. cit.,* p. 266.
5. Querido, A., *Mental Health Problems in Public Health Planning,* in Henry P. David (Ed.), *op. cit.,* p. 34.
6. *The Rockefeller Report . . .,* *op. cit.,* p. 134.

CHAPTER 11

Educational Activities

THE PLACE OF EDUCATION IN MENTAL HEALTH

ACCORDING to a report from WHO:

> In the case of nations developing mental health services, training of personnel is of first priority. Psychiatrists and psychiatric nurses must be the first trained, and their training should make them well acquainted with the principles and techniques of public health and social medicine to enable them to approach their assignment from a community-oriented viewpoint.
>
> The second echelon of personnel development will be nonmedical workers trained in work with families and community groups.
>
> The third group for training will be the attendant or aide group.[1]

In another part of the same report, this theme is continued: ". . . no new service should be set up unless adequate personnel is available for running it. Even the most efficient organization and the best physical facilities will not prevent a badly staffed service from soon becoming unsatisfactory."[2] In El Guabal, the PPSP adjusted this plan to the local needs and possibilities by organizing the educational activities at four levels: residents of psychiatry, medical students and public health doctors, public health nurses and aides and community leaders, and the general public.

TRAINING PSYCHIATRISTS

If training is defined as practical education under supervision in order to impart particular knowledge and skills which will eventually lead toward a desired change in an individual's behavior, then the first question concerns the "desired change" to be induced in psychiatrists.

According to a U.N. report:

The first problem that faces agents from outside the community. . . stems from the very fact that they are outsiders to the local communities where they work, and usually lack intimate knowledge of local conditions. Being in many cases city people, they have a particularly deficient knowledge of rural (and urban-marginal) problems. Their attitude towards the local population may be one of condescension and impatience. . . . In a survey, the most serious deficiency in project staff members was inappropriate attitudes toward the local population—rather than extent of training or knowledge of local culture. . . . Distrust of non-nationals was not considered a serious matter at all.[3]

Latin America's psychiatrists evidence a "professional complex," in which it is considered more respectable to work with the eccentricities and psychological problems of intelligent and well-off individuals than with the problems of chronic patients and lower-class groups. To "treat" this complex and to change the traditional role of psychiatrists in order to integrate them into a developing community, extra-mural work has proved to be indispensable. They will come into closer contact with other health personnel—general practitioners, specialists, social workers—and this will increase their ability to understand and handle the patient.[4]

Besides the specific work as psychiatrist in a medical center, there are three other aspects of training which can be arranged within extra-mural activities. The resident is trained to recognize and manage psychiatric patients and in scientific research. And finally, he learns to work in a team formed by people from diverse disciplines to expand his field of action.

In the PPSP, this multiple task of training the third-year resident was fulfilled through the extra-mural activities in El Guabal and Candelaria. The resident's background has been considered elsewhere (see Chapter 9).

In El Guabal, two foreign residents—one from Bolivia and another from Ecuador—received their training in social psychiatry. To become acquainted with the local population and the Medical Center, they spent their first two months *exploring the field*. The resident accompanied the assistant nurses during home visits. Since the *barrio* is small, visits could be made on foot, thus making it easier to observe environmental conditions, and at the same time to be observed by the neighbors in the company of a trusted member of the Medical Center. During these visits, with one or two exceptions, a friendly reception for, and a positive attitude toward, the new psychiatric program were evident. During each visit, the resident waited for the assistant to finish her work involving other programs of public health. Then he began informal conversations in which he explained the project, inquired about emotional and psychiatric problems, and offered specialized care. If there was the opportunity, he stressed the relation between somatic disease (for which the visit had been made) and psychological factors. By participating in this informal psychiatric interview, the assistant nurse learned how to recognize psychiatric patients who up till then had not been considered part of her work. After 15 to 20 home visits to different sections of the *barrio,* accompanied by different assistant nurses, the resident had the minimal knowledge required of living conditions and of characteristic ways of complaining about psychiatric disturbances in the community. He also learned that the role of a psychiatric patient, as well as the role of a psychiatrist, was almost unknown to these people. Most of them, including the assistant nurses, did not understand what he meant by symptoms of anxiety or depression. Consequently, they always began by talking about somatic disorders. It was obvious, however, that the patients were very interested in having an opportunity to discuss their emotional problems.

When a psychiatrist leaves the protective environment of the hospital and university to enter the field of public health, he has to face a new world and learn to live "on the other side of the fence." He is deprived of his reference group and the opportunity to share roles with professionals practicing in other specialized medical fields.

Under these circumstances, facing an "identity crisis," psychiatrists react in one of two ways. Either they suffer a *conversion* (in the sense of a religious conversion) and drop traditional psychiatric clinical procedures to promote their acceptance and prestige, or else they suffer the antithetic process of *orthodoxy,* committing themselves to the study and treatment of mental phenomena and "transference," thus isolating themselves from the rest of the staff.[5]

In El Guabal, the resident chose first to demonstrate that he was indeed a doctor, and then to demand a better acceptance of his role as a different kind of doctor.

One afternoon, two medical students came back to the center from a house call, where they had found a patient suffering from intense chest pain when breathing. The physical examination showed only slight fever but no explanation for the pain, which had forced the patient to stay in bed. Since there were no doctors in the center expect for the psychiatrist, the nurses and medical students requested his help.

Accompanied by the medical students, the psychiatrist went to see the patient. After a very careful physical examination he reached a presumptive diagnosis of viral pleurodynia, and prescribed strong analgesics. The following day, the patient had improved considerably and the psychiatrist was congratulated by everyone.

On another occasion a more dramatic situation arose. The assistant nurse in charge of the poorest and most distant section of the *barrio* arrived at the center when the psychiatrist was just about to leave at noon. Since no other doctors were there, she presented her problem to him. A recently married young woman, who had always rejected the assistant's help during pregnancy, was having serious difficulties with her first childbirth, which was being handled by a woman witchdoctor. The psychiatrist went with the head nurse and the assistant to the patient's house, which consisted of one very shabby, dark room. The patient was lying in bed, and near her stood her husband and an old, cross-eyed short woman who was asking the patient to blow into a bottle while she poured an oily liquid into the woman's vagina. The witchdoctor had injected oxytocics (certain replacement medicines) at the beginning of labor, and as a result the patient's uterus was in a state of stony contraction, and the cervix had not expanded. There was no car available to take the patient to the hospital. The psychiatrist expanded the cervix manually, and after considerable effort a baby was born with mild signs of anoxia. The psychiatrist helped him breathe. Both the mother and the witchdoctor were invited to come to the Parochial Center, the former for follow-up and the latter for obstetric training.

This event led to a better rapport between the staff and the community. Furthermore, a new family and a witchdoctor came under the control of the medical programs. These examples illustrate the need for a broad preparation in medicine as a prerequisite for introducing psychiatric programs into a community which has hitherto not heard of them. By using this indirect approach, the first step toward cooperative work was established. Afterward, integrating the mental health functions with the activities of the already-busy staff was made easier.

Joint work was the main source of new knowledge. The resident discussed and studied the public health techniques which had to be incorporated under the psychiatry program. The doctors and residents of the Department of Preventive Medicine, as well as the public health nurses, had to deal with numerous psychiatric patients who up to then had remained practically unnoticed, and were therefore in a position to discuss and study ways of treating them. At this stage, interdisciplinary discussions and social science and epidemiological publications, which are not usually strictly necessary for psychiatric training, were required. The hygienists and nurses, who do not have time to attend lectures during working hours, were encouraged to review such publications.

During the two exploratory months, the psychiatrist observed and studied the characteristics of El Guabal and the functioning of the Medical Department. Also during this period, a training program was begun for assistant nurses and medical students was instituted.

The psychiatrist opened his training in administration and research by planning an out-patient service for the patients expected to arrive after the exploratory period was over. After one year of extra-mural experience, the resident had learned not only new concepts of public health and administration, but also was motivated to learn more about social psychiatry and to orient his work to the service of the those groups which needed more of his specialized knowledge.

The essential change from traditional psychiatry lies in the study and handling of the society in which the mental illnesses occur instead of concern for the pathological behavior of one individual.

In Candelaria, the PPSP started its functions in July 1968, one year later than in El Guabal. Although the Department of Psychiatry of the School of Medicine had been occasionally sending some patients to Candelaria since 1965, formal and regular activities in social psychiatry were not established until 1968 when a third-year resident, who also had a master's degree in public health, was sent there.

This resident had formerly been the director of the Medical Center, so he had a thorough knowledge of the people and the community. Furthermore, because of his experience in both public health and psychiatry, he was able to organize the PPSP in a more difficult environment than El Guabal—that is to say, in a larger rural population.

This example illustrates how professional people with special skills can best be utilized. However, because there are few psychiatrists with public health training anywhere, a report from WHO considers it essential to stimulate interest among young psychiatrists, for example, by adding courses on epidemiology and social anthropology to their post-graduate training program.

TRAINING MEDICAL STUDENTS AND PHYSICIANS

The objective at this level is to give students a closer identification with the tasks and purposes of mental health, and to encourage them to self-assess their role in helping people protect themselves against pathogenic factors in the environment.[6] In the PPSP it was considered crucial to show students to what extent their own attitudes in dealing with patients and their families is a significant factor not only in preventing psychiatric problems, but also in their success or failure as physicians. The preventive possibilities of the physician derive mostly from his understanding of the human being as an individual and as a member of social groups. The medical student must also be taught to appreciate his role as an educator, particularly where the promotion of mental health is concerned and in relation to family environment and community attitudes toward mental disorders.

Mental health promotion can never be made effective by a psychiatrist alone. Mental hygiene will remain an empty promise if the general practitioner is not enabled to act as its main agent in the community.[7] In those geographic regions were psychiatric consultants are scarce—as is the case in most areas of Latin America—a student must also learn that he will have significant responsibility for the psychiatric treatment of his future patients. He must be alerted to the psychotherapeutic opportunities which occur from moment to moment in his relationships with patients and the community, especially at times of crises. A student must be prepared to help ease the environmental tension surrounding his patients. He must know who in the community can aid him in his task—for instance, the public health nurse and the clergyman. And last he has to be informed about the realistic limitations of psychiatric treatment and prevention, lest he become disillusioned early in his future practice.[8]

In El Guabal this level of training was directed toward the sixth-year student of medicine, the clerk who spends one month in the extra-mural centers of the School of Medicine. As noted earlier, the clerks have already had three courses in psychiatry as well as field work in the barrios. Each student is assigned to one family in the *barrio* during his third year to act as tutor to the family in health matters for three years.

With such a background, the clerks were considered ready to start dealing with psychiatric patients in the community as the principal associate of the psychiatrist. During their one-month shift in El Guabal, the clerks were in charge of most of the psychiatric interviews and medication of psychiatric patients under the close supervision of the resident, who discussed with them each case. When requested, the resident carried out a brief interview, which the student attended, of patients not easily understood by the clerks.

Here again, this routine was gradually introduced in order to avoid interference with the other, usually overloaded, medical programs. At the beginning of the PPSP, with few psychiatric patients, the resident was able to take care of all of them, especially during the exploratory period. In this way, the doctors and nurses in El Guabal were used to seeing mental patients as a regular part of their out-patient service. After a few months, it was easy to transfer care of these patients to the students already taking care of other somatic patients. By the end of the second year of PPSP's activities in El Guabal, medical students were working in the field of psychiatry from 24 to 32 hours per month, according to the number of students on monthly turn, which was two or three.

Students received instruction and supervision in writing summarized psychiatric histories and evaluation notes focused on the principal areas of conflict in individual and family behavior. The first interview with new patients was usually attended by the supervisor resident. He also held special meetings with the group of new clerks who arrived monthly to discuss basic instructions about the techniques of psychiatric interviews, psychiatric histories, and diagnosis and treatment fitted to the routines of the Medical Center. Each clerk also made at least one psychiatric house call to handle emergencies and to observe the interaction of patients with their families and the neighborhood.

The most exciting innovation involving the medical students during the second year of the PPSP in El Guabal was two lectures they gave to the parents of the *barrio* on sexual adjustment in marriage as a part of a series to educate the public. These lectures aroused interest and confidence. Countless questions reflecting psychological and cultural problems were answered by the students while the resident in psychiatry observed.

Public health doctors working in El Guabal were trained to promote mental health amid the activities of any medical program, as well as in the therapeutic possibilities of early treatment and diagnosis of problems. The PPSP thus contributes to the development of a wider conception of the tasks of public health.

In Candelaria, during the year of activities in social psychiatry reported in this work, the clerks worked two hours weekly with psychiatric patients under the supervision of the resident. The resident also discussed with the clerks psychiatric emergencies and chemotherapy in weekly seminars of one hour each.

The psychiatrist in charge at Candelaria, as an expert in public health, used to participate actively in the public health seminars which take place once a week in the School of Medicine in Cali, with the assistance of the staff, students of the Department of Preventive Medicine, and the School of Sanitary Engineering of the university and representatives of the local authorities.

TRAINING ALLIED PERSONNEL

This category includes public health assistant nurses and student nurses. In Cali, as in the rest of Colombia, there is a shortage of psychiatric nurses. All of them work in the psychiatric hospital. Therefore, it was necessary to do without them, at least during the initial period of the project.

The public health nurse has over the last two or three decades played a major part in the great advances made in social and preventive medicine. In the mother and child services, in the school health services, in the prevention of communicable diseases, much of the progress has been due to her patient and persistent efforts in educating individuals and groups. The public health nurse is a welcome visitor in whom the family places great confidence. Thus, she has an important part to play in advising on such problems as the presence of chronic somatic or psychiatric diseases, in helping during times of crises, and in improving the psychological understanding between generations and different cultures which meet in marginal zones in Latin American cities. She can promote mentally healthy attitudes in mothers toward their babies, sometimes even during and before pregnancy. For all these activities a public health nurse needs, however, special preparation and education.[9] Only recently, in Cali, psychiatric training has been introduced whereby student nurses are taught the elementary principles of mental hygiene and receive instruction in nursing patients suffering from mental disorders.

To explain the educational activities of allied health personnel in El Guabal and Candelaria, a few concepts from a WHO report will be mentioned.[10] Within a medical center in a community, nurses and assistant nurses are the buttresses of services, assisting in the application of treatments and living with day-to-day responsibility for patients. Nurses should ensure liaison between psychiatrists and patients and act as a link between the patient and his family. Finally, the nurse can carry out effective educational work in the community and within the family.

Nurses and assistants, who are drawn from a cross-section of society, should be utilized to the fullest in making contact with patients.

Public health nurses and assistants must receive training to help them understand their own behavior and that of those around them. There should be adequate instruction in the attitudes to be adopted toward pathological behavior on the part of patients. A nurse also needs to know something about re-education and rehabilitation techniques. Theory and practice must be developed together side by side. Thus, training in small groups, according to the principles of group dynamics, is necessary.

In El Guabal, the 8 public health assistants in charge of the different programs of the Medical Department in the St. John the Baptist Parochial Center had completed at least 5 years of primary education, and most of them also had 2 or 3 years of high school. All had passed a one-year course to be certified as assistant nurses and another course which qualified them as public health assistants. Their monthly salary was around $65 (U.S.). Some were married and had children. They came from the same low social strata as the population of El Guabal, so they shared common attitudes and beliefs regarding mental illness with the public.

A questionnaire exploring these attitudes was given to the assistants during the resident's exploratory period. It was found that the concepts relative to mental disorder were closely linked with the cultural beliefs of the population. For instance, the most frequent causes of psychiatric diseases were thought to be evil spells or witchcraft, masturbation, and excessive study, although the persons who gave the replies had considerable experience in the field of public health. Psychiatric terms were little known, as shown by a choice of false answers to describe examples of depression, phobia, and anxiety, as well as for more difficult questions regarding the use of electroencephalography, the seriousness of schizophrenic diagnosis, and the approximate frequency of psychosis in the general population. The replies given the first time reflected a tolerant and positive attitude toward learning difficulties in children and personality problems in adults. On the other hand, the general attitude was negative regarding psychotics, since the replies chosen to indicate the characteristic signs of madness were aggressiveness or uncontrolled sexuality. The relation between biological factors and mental disease was unclear in the minds of the assistants. Psychiatric hospitalization did not elicit rejection since it was accepted that a patient eventually would be discharged.

In most cases, heredity was regarded as the principal cause of psychiatric disease. The common attitude of the population and assistants was shown in different ways early in the exploratory period of the PPSP. For example, a young woman who had been married for a few months and had recently arrived at the district, had suffered from acute psychosis during the first days of the puerperal period and had tried to kill her own son. The patient was hospitalized at the San Isidro Hospital before the psychiatry program at El Guabal was started. When she came home after two months, she was received with hostility by her neighbors and by her husband, who wanted to leave her. The assistant nurse who visited this family supported this attitude, labeling the patient as a criminal mother and, therefore, sanctioning the husband's wish to leave her. When the psychiatric activities started, the resident discussed the case with the assistant nurse. She became more tolerant and transmitted this attiude to the community, based on the certainty that the young woman's psychotic outburst was over.

In order to change attitudes as well as to train the assistants in mental health activities, both theortical and practical teaching was initiated at El Guabal. As their knowledge advanced, these workers asked the resident for psychiatric help for themselves or their families.

One assistant reacted toward her husband's unemployment with insomnia, anorexia, frequent crying, and lack of interest in her work. She received anti-depressive medicine and improved in a few weeks.

Another assistant had a 55-year old aunt who was anxious and sad. The family was very much worried because the aunt was losing weight and looked very ill. This patient did not belong to the *barrio,* so the assistant was advised to take her aunt to San Isidro Psychiatric Hospital. She did not. Shortly afterward, the aunt committed suicide.

Naturally, these cases impressed the staff. All the assistants and even the nurses sought consultation about minor emotional difficulties, but the resident had to take care of other activities of the PPSP.

However, this situation presented a unique opportunity to improve the assistants' training. Ari Querido states that, "For the hard-core worker, who has the same culture as the people receiving psychiatric care, teaching must give a systematic awareness of his own experience."[11]

Perdomo observed in Cali that the majority of students who request a psychiatric interview at the Universidad del Valle come from the School of Nursing or the School of Medicine, probably because the contact they have with psychiatry there gives them a greater degree of "mental disease awareness."[12] The same thing happens with an assistant nurse in the field of public health who comes in contact with psychiatry for the first time.

The last assumption was supported by the concern displayed by nurses and assistants at the Parochial Center over new mental patients whose sickness had up to then been concealed.

During the sceond year of PPSP in El Guabal, a "group of human relations" was established which met for 90 minutes once a week. Assistants and nurses met under the supervision of the resident to gain insight into the dynamics of their own behavior and their reactions in handling patients and dealing with personal problems. Their training was completed with lectures and demonstrations.

The questionnaire already mentioned, on attitudes toward and knowledge of psychiatry, showed initially that only 38.5 per cent of the answers—out of 350—were correct. After a course of 10 weekly lectures given by the resident, the questionnaire was repeated and 73.3 per cent of the answers were correct.

To demonstrate psychiatric symptoms, a group of last-year students at the School of Nursing of the Universidad del Valle gave a series of four lectures using attractive visual material. Another group of post-graduate nurses enacted sociodramas to demonstrate the recognition and adequate handling of anxiety, depression, agitation, and dementia.

After this theoretical teaching, in February 1968 each assistant received an assignment to visit a family with psychiatric patients two or more times a week and to discuss these visits with the psychiatrist. The following are examples of this practice.

The first assistant went to the house of two schizophrenic sisters, 20 and 25 years old, living with their mother but not their father, and a sister, who worked in a hospital. One of the patients had a medical history of four periods of acute psychosis, during which she ran away from home, became pregnant, and finally went to the psychiatric hospital where she improved after two or three months of treatment with drugs and electric-shock therapy. The other patient usually remained at home to help her mother with housework and to take care of the children of the first patient. She had also been hospitalized in San Isidro, five times, because she had shown signs of apathy, fretfulness, and complete indifference toward her environment. In February 1968, both patients were unbalanced, the first agitated and aggressive, the second inactive. Both rejected help from the assistant nurse, but with the family's cooperation it was finally possible to convince the patients to accept the parental application of Prolixin (Fluphenazine Enanthate), after which the symptoms diminished greatly. During the following four months, the patients received the Prolixin injection every two or three weeks, and an anti-parkinson drug. The advantages of this treatment were obvious to the staff of the parochial center and the community. In the first case, running away and resultant pregnancy and hospitalization were avoided. Perhaps most important was the attitude of the community toward the patients' change; they were no longer labeled as "crazy women."

The second assistant nurse was in charge of two patients, a 22-year-old man and a 36-year-old woman. Both were single and had been suffering from very frequent grand mal convulsions for the last 15 years. The two patients were worn out, incapable of controlling their sphincter muscles, and were a burden to their families. Since the patients lived near each other, both families helped to control the convulsions of either patient by pressing the middle finger of the left hand, the "heart finger," of the patient. Drugs had never been used. The assistant nurse gave an anti-convulsive drug to the two families and checked its application. In a few days the patients were free from seizures and could help carry out some household duties. After a month, a prescription was given for the drugs (formerly provided free), but thereafter neither of the patients received the drug again, and both relapsed. This development is probably due to tradition and poverty, both of which are characterized by resignation to a fate which renders such problems insoluble. It is certain that both families could not afford to buy the drug, but the fact is that they passively accepted its removal. This attitude of inert resignation could not be changed solely by the results of the treatment. The family and the community required active attention to motivate them to care for their charges more adequately.

Another assistant was in charge of a 34-year-old mother of three small children with whom she lived in a rented room near the Parochial Center. Her husband had been working in another city for three months. Her neighbors went to the center to report that she had suddenly started screaming and tearing her clothes off like a mad woman. The resident in psychiatry went with the assistant to the woman's home where the patient showed signs of agitation and confusion. The assistant gave her an intramuscular injection of chloropormazine, which quickly put her to sleep. The neighbors were asked to watch over her that night, and thereafter the assistant visited her daily until it was possible for the husband to return. The recovery was complete, and the diagnosis was dissociative reaction.

The five cases just described illustrate medical care given to psychiatric patients within the community, using staff without any degrees and with no experience in this field. Each assistant gave the drug prescribed by the doctor, checked its proper use, and supplied simple support psychotherapy which was facilitated in these cases by the good relationship already established through other programs of the Medical Department. Special emphasis was placed on showing the assistants useful techniques of intervention in times of crisis. After one month's work with model patients, the assistants' confidence increased when they began having direct contact with real patients. Subsequently, the checking and follow-up care of patients already registered under the Pilot Plan of Social Psychiatry was organized. The basic method was the home calls made by the assistant nurses under other programs of the Medical Department. Beginning in March 1968, the assistants were assigned one morning each week for home calls to psychiatric patients.

Calls were made from Monday to Friday for treatment and control of patients. During the three years prior to the PPSP, the number of visits was 3,963 in 1964, 10,769 in 1965, and 11,378 in 1966. The stabilization of the figures shows that this service was probably being used at full capacity. However, after these visits were organized to cover psychiatric patients, 457 psychiatric visits were made by the assistants from July 1968 to June 1969.

Also during the second year in El Guabal, besides the group meetings with the assistants, the resident discussed the home calls with assistants and medical students, demonstrating some easy techniques of interrogatory and supportive psychotherapy with a few cooperative patients.

In Candelaria lectures and demonstrations were given by the resident and a psychiatric nurse from San Isidro Psychiatric Hospital to student assistant nurses, and a full-time assistant was hired to take care of new psychiatric patients.

EDUCATING THE PUBLIC

Of critical importance in the promotion of mental health is dissemination of information to community leaders and the public aimed at promoting active participation in the program. This requires education rather than merely information.[13] Centers like El Guabal or Candelaria, where some technical services and other facilities are centralized, can be effective media for programs of public education, thanks to their easy accessibility and their outstanding position at the local level. According to WHO, in planning an information and education program, those to be reached may be considered in three categories, the objectives for each being somewhat different. The basic principle of operation, however, is common to all three groups and must therefore be stressed at the outset. The person who undertakes to conduct a program must not only be well-prepared professionally, but, in speaking to other professional groups as an authority, must confine himself to his competence in the mental health field. This prevents his undermining his authority by identifying with or intruding upon the disciplines of his listeners.

Group I is composed of laymen who are likely to be called upon to help those in trouble and who are sometimes called the "caretakers" of society. They are teachers, police officers, clergymen, members of the legal profession—judges and lawyers—and in some rural areas, the native healers. Obviously, they must be well informed regarding resources in the community to which they can turn.[14]

Group II, called the "gatekeepers," comprises those people in the community who are pivotal in shaping attitudes. Among them are union leaders, local politicians, and those concerned with the mass media—the press, radio, television, and cinema. The educator must convince them of what mental health education can accomplish, as the media are most effective in creating an atmosphere conducive to change.[15]

Group III consists of the general public. Parents—particularly of younger children in Latin American communities—are highly motivated to ensure the healthy development of their offspring. A program directed to this group has to be easily understood. At least as much harm can be done by misinformation or by misunderstanding of accurate information as may arise from withholding information altogether.

In El Guabal, education at the public level was addressed mainly to the first and third groups, since the *barrio* is served by the "gatekeepers" from the larger city of Cali.

The "caretakers" were educated mainly by social workers from the parochial center. In other medical centers the social workers are usually included within the medical programs, but in El Guabal they constitute a separate department and were first to be contacted regarding marital or employment maladjustments and adolescent problems. During the second year of PPSP, the social workers began to use the new techniques of consultation and referral. Some cases were treated directly by the social worker under the supervision of the psychiatrist.

The parish priest also referred adolescents to the psychiatrist during the second year. Finally, the police were once called to help the psychiatrist with a psychotic woman. The next day one assistant returned to the patient's home accompanied by a policeman, whose presence was enough for the patient to accept an injection of a transquilizer (Prolixin—1cc). Since then the patient has cooperated.

In the first year of the PPSP, five lectures were given for grammar school teachers, which were attended by 14 teachers from several institutions. Before the lectures, the same questionnaire which had been taken by the assistant nurses was given to the teachers. The answers were similar in both groups, confirming the supposition that both came from similar socio-cultural environments. Again the rate of correct answers was over one-third of the total—38.5 per cent for teachers and 38.6 per cent for assistants—indicating that knowledge about mental illness was independent in these groups from occupation. The lectures covered the following topics in May 1968: a) growth and maturation from birth to adolescence, b) attitudes toward children, and c) psychopathology at school age and adolescence. During the second year, several teachers referred children to the PPSP, or they asked for guidance in handling their students, and occasionally for their own problems.

In addition, the psychiatrist gave, during the first year, 2 courses of 5 lectures organized by the social workers for 2 groups of parents. More than 200 people received a certificate for having attended all the lectures. The lectures paved the way for more direct communication, especially through the home visits of assistant nurses and medical students. Both groups of parents attended the following lectures: a) growth of the child, b) child psychopathology, c) adolescence, d) normal sexual behavior, and e) marital adjustment.

During the second year in El Guabal, the resident gave the lectures about growth and psychopathology of children and the medical students gave the lectures about sexual behavior, arousing keen interest and some questioning from the audience. For example, a mother asked the following: "I would like to know why I feel no pleasure and only rage during sexual relations." Another one asked why "there is no orgasm, although I want it to happen very much." Many expressed fear of becoming pregnant if they had "full relations" with their husbands, or said they practiced *coitus interruptus* to avoid conception. The belief that sexual relations without orgasm are generally infertile is widely held. There were also questions regarding impotency and sexual indifference in husbands. In one case, it was said that the husband "felt pain and his stomach swelled whenever he had sexual relations." An almost total lack of foreplay appeared frequent, giving rise to frustration, particularly in women.

The following are examples of the questions about children directed to the psychiatrist:

"Why does a four-year-old boy suck his thumb?"

"Should a five-year-old girl be weaned, even by harsh methods?"

"Is it good to protect the newborn from 'mal ojo'?"[15a]

"Why does a healthy child show sexual curiosity?"

These examples reflect a positive attitude toward the PPSP. In fact, after two years the public in El Guabal accepted the help offered by the psychiatrist and were now open to changes that will enable the next generation to take more advantage of medical science.

In Candelaria 5 lectures were given to an audience of 12

teachers about psychological problems of school children. Another 5 lectures were attended by 10 mothers. The Medical Center has found it difficult to involve the community in educational activties regarding public health. Because it is a rural community and people are scattered, education should be directed toward leaders of Group II, the "gatekeepers"—landlords, employers, and local authorities. In fact, this approach was used to increase the receptivity of a prevalence survey through interviews with the priest, the mayor, the leaders of community councils, and teachers in November 1968. After this indirect education, the survey was made without resistance from March through May 1969.

NOTES

1. WHO, *Technical Report Series*, No. 223, p. 17.
2. *Ibid.*, p. 23.
3. U.N., *1965 World Social Situation*, p. 35.
4. WHO, *Technical Report Series*, No. 223, p. 24.
5. Perry, E. S., "Observations on Social Processes in Psychiatric Research," in Bergen, B. J., and Thomas, C. S. (Eds.), *Issues and Problems in Social Psychiatry: A Book of Readings*, Springfield, Illinois, Charles C Thomas, 1966.
6. WHO, *Technical Report Series*, No. 185, p. 19.
7. *Ibid.*, No. 208, pp. 6–8.
8. *Ibid.*, pp. 21–23.
9. *Ibid.*, No. 223, pp. 30–31.
10. *Ibid.*, pp. 25–26.
11. Querido, *loc. cit.*
12. Perdomo, R., *Utilizacion del Servicio Psiquiatrico Estudiantil en la Universidad del Valle*, V Congreso APAL, Bogotá, 1968 (mimeograph).
13. WHO, *Technical Report Series*, No. 223, p. 32.
14. *Ibid.*, pp. 32–36.
15. U.N., *1965 World Social Situation*, p. 17.
15a. I.e., *mal de ojo*, or evil eye.

CHAPTER 12

Organizational Activities

ORGANIZATION OF FUNCTIONS

ORGANIZATION of the PPSP had two main objectives. The first was to integrate teamwork and the second was to differentiate and interrelate specific functions for each individual involved.

According to Ari Querido, most activities constituting mental health care programs are not necessarily identical with an equal number of specialists or specific institutions. The expert worker can carry out, supervise, and advise on a number of different functions, each representing an item in the program.[1] This concept is particularly relevant to the PPSP as a demonstration project aiming to meet the psychiatric needs of a population with exigious resources, both human and physical, as certainly would be the situation elsewhere in Latin America.

To organize the teamwork with its numerous functions, certain prerequisites had to be fulfilled:[2]

1) The local organization had to be integrated with higher levels (district, provincial or departmental, national). Higher level guidance was necessary for technical information: indications of resources available, clarification of choices and possibilities and suggestions regarding feasible innovations and enlargements. The PPSP depended on the Department of Psychiatry of the Universidad del Valle, which is connected to higher national and international institutions, for these objectives.

2) The local population had to meet with the psychiatrists in order to arrive at a consensus on needs and objectives. With the medical centers already functioning in El Guabal and Candelaria, the necessary structure was established.

3) Training of personnel and a study of the locality were necessary.

INTEGRATION OF TEAMWORK

According to a report from WHO, "The team approach to problems is difficult to arrange. However, the rewards to be reaped make the effort well worthwhile."[3]

In order to establish multi-disciplinary mental health teams, two considerations are necessary: the selection of an appropriate team leader, and the selection and organization of the individuals who will serve as his teammates.

In the field of mental health, the leader must be an authority in his own field. As we have seen, the third-year resident of psychiatry in Cali had enough training to solve most of the problems to be met in the practice of his specialty.

He also has to be an able administrator and coordinator to strengthen the cohesion of the team. This means that he must be an expert in handling human relations. The resident in Cali had available the close and constant supervision of the psychiatrists on the staff of the Department of Psychiatry of the Universidad del Valle.

The leader must be a person of integrity who respects his teammates. In Cali, candidates are carefully screened before being admitted as residents in psychiatry.

The selection of team members is no less important for the success of the psychiatric unit. The main qualifications demanded of team members are adequate preparation, high motivation, emotional warmth, health, and intelligence.

Moreover, in developing programs for extra-mural care, the skills of "outside helpers" such as teachers, clergymen, and employers must be readily available and they should be given a clear sense of participating in the task of helping those who are or may become mentally disturbed. There should be easy channels of communication between "the helpers" and the psychiatric unit.

A pyramidal structure evolved in El Guabal, with the resident of psychiatry at its peak and the community at its base. At the intermediary levels, the highest status was accorded the public health doctors and medical students. Next came the public health nurses, and occasionally nursing students. Third were the assistant nurses. Then came the "outside helpers"—teachers, the priest, policemen, and volunteers. And finally, there were the parents and the whole community.

In this system we see that the higher the status, the more specialized and difficult the training, and the smaller the number of persons directly involved. Since their training is simple and rapid, a wide diffusion of the activities at the lower levels may be attained progressively.

TEAMWORK FUNCTIONS

In the pyramidal structure just described, the psychiatrist must be in a position that allows his specific aptitudes to be used to the advantage of the lower levels, through advice, consultation, supervision, teaching, and direct treatment of special cases. At the other extreme, the staff at the lower levels—which includes most people —will be in charge of the initial contact with patients, will send them to the Medical Department, and will even provide medical care for the average patient within the community.

The intermediary level serves as a bridge between the two extremes and will develop the therapeutic activities which do not require the more complex techniques of the specialist, but do entail a closer and constant contact with the patient and his family.

In other words, the psychiatrist leads and the other members of the team are responsible for the direct care of patients, as well as for gathering data from the community. Functions other than leadership were carried out through psychiatric interviews in the St. John the Baptist Parochial Center and during the home visits made by the assistant nurses. An out-patient service for psychiatric patients was arranged by the public health nurses and doctors, with minimum disruption of other medical services.

Psychiatric interviews for registration, history taking, and treatment of patients were carried out by medical students, supervised by the resident, Tuesday afternoons and Friday mornings. Although the psychiatrist was in charge of most of these interviews at the beginning, he later functioned mainly as a supervisor and took care of a few special patients who, after being adequately diagnosed, were referred to students for treatment and follow-up. After the two-month exploratory period, the PPSP personnel in six months—from October 1, 1967 to March 31, 1968—recorded a total of 110 interviews, 49 with new patients and 61 for treatment and follow-up. These figures totaled 181, of which 54 were new, during the semester from January 2, 1969 to June 30, 1969.

The duration of the interviews varied. If the pathology of a case was obvious, as in grand mal epilepsy or serious mental retardation, the medical interview was limited to prescribing medication and giving full explanations about its usage. In cases of emotional and personality disturbances, the interviews lasted longer to permit the case to be studied and to provide supportive psychotherapy.

In any event, the patients were given a future appointment, the timing of which depended on their needs, in order to control the patients' progress. The patients were also assigned to the assistant nurse in charge of home calls in the coresponding area. Once the pertinent information was included in the medical history, an individual card was filled out and a pin placed on the map of the *barrio* to make it possible to find the patient easily.

As has been pointed out, each medical history was filed under a code number for each house. El Guabal is divided into blocks designated with letters from A to CL, each block having various numbered houses. Therefore, in the files of the Medical Department, case history AY23 corresponded to house number 23 in block AY. This history included the demographical and medical data of all the individuals under any medical program. The information from psychiatric interviews was to be added to this history. Individual cards with the file number and epidemiological data were arranged alphabetically. Also, as mentioned, a district map was prepared on which every patient was represented by a pin placed in the place corresponding to his house. Diagnosis was indicated on the map by using different colored pins. A red pin in AY 23 space indicated that in that house there was a schizophrenic. A yellow pin in the same space meant that a psycho-neurotic patient also lived there.

El Guabal patients received medical care by appointments previously given them by the assistant nurse during the home visit, or by the doctor. Emergency cases were handled immediately. New patients were registered and assigned under a specific program after evaluation. The Medical Department as well as the PPSP also sent doctors or medical students to the homes of patients requiring home care.

The consultation fee was equivalent to 50 cents (U.S.) (eight Colombian pesos), and was slightly higher in case of a house call. The patients could buy drugs at reduced prices at the Parochial Center Discount Store.

If a patient required special treatment such as EEG or psychological tests, he was referred to the San Isidro Psychiatric Hospital. On one occasion a suicidal patient was hospitalized. After three weeks he was able to continue his care at home.

The usual out-patient care consisted of prescribing drugs, superficial psychotherapy, and assistance with social problems, such as employment, family planning, or marital difficulties. The doctor tried to solve the immediate problem using the proper drugs or the facilities of other programs of the department. This saved time, and the mental and somatic patient became simply a patient of the Medical Department. In turn, the psychiatrist and the hygienist were accepted as persons who were ready to help in any health problem. Thus, it was possible to avoid labeling a mental patient as someone special and abnormal.

At El Guabal, emphasis was placed on supportive psychotherapy and environment manipulation rather than intensive insight therapy.

LEADERSHIP FUNCTIONS

The leader exercises authority and acts as a link with the other members of the community. By providing useful resources, he obtains a greater degree of influence and respect. Consequently, leadership is an active and variable process involving various functions of the leader and his followers.

Leaders may be spontaneous—i.e., determined by common consensus—or assigned. In El Guabal, leadership was assigned by the university to the resident of psychiatry. This assignment added to the psychiatrist leader's responsibilities for individual treatment of mental patients. Various non-medical activities in management and social fields proved to be an inherent source of conflict between his role as doctor and that as manager or leader. The hygienist as well as the social psychiatrist has to operate in four different capacities: health manager, public official, doctor, and community leader.

The resident met these demands as follows:

1) *The doctor,* in a population which had not heard about psychiatry, was expected to alleviate all kinds of complaints. Although he used to be introduced as "specialist in mental and nervous diseases," he had to act as internist and obstetrician, as has been reported elsewhere.

2) *The manager and public official,* who belongs to a bureaucratic organization, had to attend various social activities such as delivering degrees and diplomas to women of the district who had completed cooking, hairstyling, and dressmaking courses under the Community Promotion Program of the Medical Department, or granting certificates to fathers who attended the family education courses organized by the Welfare Department. On these occasions,

the resident delivered the degrees and certificates to each person, jointly with the doctor, director of the medical department, and head nurse. These events were attended by the families and friends of those who received diplomas.

The importance of such public performances lies in the traditional significance of paternalistic authority and the demands of personal dependency on the *patron,* which have been analyzed in the first part of this work. Also, as a manager the resident presented several reports to the medical staff of the Departments of Preventive Medicine and of Psychiatry of the Universidad del Valle, as well as to the directors of *Fundacion Hernando Carvajal,* since these three institutions supplied financial and technical aid to the Medical Department.

Moreover, a report on the activities of the psychiatry program was presented to two members of the International Committee Against Mental Illness, who traveled from the United States to observe the development of the PPSP, which is supported by this international agency.

The manager and public official also must intercede as representative of the community and, in the case of mental patients, in the external relations with other groups and higher authorities. He must avoid the mental patient's being labeled "crazy" within the community, for example, or utilize external sources to improve psychiatric services, or to make them cheaper.

3) *Leader of the community* was educator, promoter and advisor for mental health activities in the community.

As a process of interaction, leadership can be accomplished in different ways, depending on the social distance between leader and followers. The rather close interaction with the hard-core staff working in the community is called *supervision.*

Another type of leadership is the interaction with professionals and non-professionals who work to serve the community but are not subordinate to the psychiatrist under the program. This leadership is called *psychiatric consultation,* and is a way to expand or increase the scope and effectiveness of scarce professionals. The consultant requests the psychiatrist's help to understand and deal better with the mental problems of an individual or a group. The psychiatrist must facilitate the consultant's work without encouraging dependency or pretending to dominate him.

The importance of the consultation will be better understood by bearing in mind the psychiatric problems of the community which do not directly reach the psychiatrist. Greenblat[4] points out that in the United States, 1 of every 7 adult persons seeks psychiatric help some time in their lives, especially for problems relative to personal adjustment, marriage, or children. Of these individuals, 42 per cent call on religious leaders, 29 per cent on general doctors, and 11 per cent on other agencies. Only 18 per cent see a psychiatrist. In Latin American countries, the proportion of persons with mental health problems who see a psychiatrist is obviously even lower. Therefore, it is the psychiatrist's responsibility to acknowledge, accept, and support the help that may be provided by priests, general doctors, teachers, advisors, and even witchdoctors. They may detect preliminary symptoms in patients, request psychiatric consultation, give information, and participate in the treatment and rehabilitation of most patients within the community and family group.

Finally, the third type of leadership is that of the *executive planner,* which does not require interpersonal relations with other members of the community.

In conclusion, the image of the psychiatrist, who leads certain activities directed to the community, has multiple facets, which may lead to ambiguity. This ambiguity may exist even among workers in the field of social psychiatry, when, for instance, the question arises regarding the psychiatrist's role in the organization of financial matters or in the integration of activities to coordinate and harmonize personnel relations in a medical center. These uncertainties reflect the present stage of development of social psychiatry and community psychiatry, which may seem more complex owing to the experiments and changes to which they are subject.

At El Guabal, the resident remained in close contact with the university and was, therefore, able to maintain his professional identity as leader. The social psychiatrist must handle the difficulties of development, "fraternal rivalry," and "maternal dependence."

The perfectionist urge to have complete knowledge of each

case in order to institute long-term psychotherapy is replaced by the wish to increase the resources which will reach the majority of the people. Consequently, the therapist must take command of human and material resources. The social psychiatrist directs his attention to the needs and values of the general public and to public health. But a really useful and innovative program of social psychiatry must enjoy the necessary freedom to develop its own concepts and psychiatric techniques. This means that the social psychiatrist is above all a public health official.

NOTES

1. Querido, a, *loc. cit.*
2. U.N., *1965 World Social Situation,* pp. 37–38.
3. WHO, *Technical Report Series,* No. 223, p. 36.
4. Greenblat, Milton, "Mental Health Consultation," in Freedman and Kaplan (Eds.), *op. cit.,* p. 1558.

CHAPTER **13**

Research

THE NEED FOR RESEARCH

RESEARCH is defined as a systematic inquiry into, or a careful examination of, a subject in order to discover or revise facts, theories, applications and so on. We wish to emphasize the word *systematic,* which presupposes an order, plan, or method.

In psychiatry, research is crucial because, according to Jaspers,

> There are very few, perhaps no, assertions which are not somewhere and at sometime under dispute. . . . Not only assertions, but methods themselves come under dispute and it is quite an achievement if two investigators will agree upon method and only argue over their actual findings. Compared with this situation, somatic research in psychiatry at present pursues a relatively firm and smooth path. . . . If (social psychiatrists) wish to place their statements and discoveries on firm ground, above the daily flood of psychological notions, we shall almost always be forced to reflect on our methodology. . . . In the face of outside criticism

we are forced to defend ourselves and clarify our own position. A science in dispute must first of all show its merits by factual results but, particularly when these are not so readily accessible, we must anticipate some criticism of the methods we employ.[1]

What can we expect from our methods? Jaspers says,

They should help us to gain new ground and enrich our knowledge in depth while they widen our experience: they should enable us to understand cause and effect and they should indicate to us comprehensible relationships, the verification of which is tied to our presuppositions. They should not involve us with what are mere logical possibilities divorced from observation and experience, and their value should show itself in the extent to which we can assess and influence events that arise from our contact with persons.[2]

Two prerequisites for methodological knowledge are obvious from these quotations—first, observation of reality and, second, criticism of methods and observations in order to test findings. Another prerequisite is a broad training in clinical psychiatry ". . . in order to prevent the specialist from developing a private language and mode of thought so he can no longer communicate with his psychiatric colleagues."[3]

Any plan aiming to introduce innovations reaching not only specialists but also the wider public and the community necessitates a firm body of knowledge, so that the new plan can relate to similar disciplines on an equal basis. Also, some way of conducting research on an international level is a necessary next step.

To attain the desired goal of social psychiatry in Latin America, that is to say, to uncover social factors as clues to the onset, course, and outcome of mental illness and the adequate organization of community care, research must be done, especially in the field of epidemiology and then in such areas as rapid social change, ecology, malnutrition, and other problems of socio-economic development—unemployment, poor housing, poverty, illiteracy,—as well as in mental health promotion and administration,

In the PPSP, systematic training in research methods is not yet organized, but the third-year resident is encouraged to work along with more experienced research workers from the staff of the Department of Psychiatry of the Universidad del Valle.

The research in social psychiatry during the initial two years of the PPSP in Cali carried out by the residents in charge trained the specialists in the epidemiological methodology of mental disorders.

The shortage of staff trained in scientific methodology, and the scarcity of accurate epidemiological data, are regarded as a crucial obstacle to the improvement of mental health in Latin America. Therefore, it is recommended that every psychiatrist have training in research, although to demand of each resident a piece of independent research is, according to a WHO report, "highly unrealistic."[4]

Some of the research activities done by the residents in Cali will be presented, mainly as an illustration of the kind of exposure to the problems of scientific research which will encourage research-oriented work during professional practice.

THE EPIDEMIOLOGICAL APPROACH

The importance of the epidemiological approach in the study of psychiatric disorders has become increasingly apparent during the last two decades. A WHO report sums up this situation:

Effective prevention of mental disorders must be based on accurate knowledge about prevalence and incidence and on reliable information about the absolute and relative weight of various causal factors. . . . One of the most promising ways of obtaining such data [is] through the study of the mass aspects of diseases and the comparative investigation of disease distribution in time and space, [that is to say] the epidemiology of mental disorders.[5]

The epidemiological methodology in psychiatry can be used for two, partly interrelated, purposes. First, what has been called "operational research" can elicit facts about treated and untreated disease in the community which are needed for the intelligent planning and administration of psychiatric services. This type of approach is clearly of special importance in those areas with inadequate psychiatric services, as in Latin American countries. Public health administrators must have estimates of both present and future demands for psychiatric services, and these requirements differ according to geographical conditions, social organization, and the age and structure of particular populations. Moreover, they must study the functional efficiency of psychiatric services, existing or planned, in relation to these demands.

Second, epidemiological methods can also be used in clinical work, to seek clues to the causes of disease. The comparison of the diseases of population groups in relation to various factors —time, sex, age, occupation, social situation—should allow the comparing of similar groups. In this way, it may be possible to identify the groups which are particularly affected and to suggest etiological factors, which might explain specific susceptibility to diseases, or the forms in which they are manifested. When such factors can be changed, methods of disease control can be tested in the field. This second approach is of less immediate utility than operational research, but in the long run, its practical importance may be even greater. In fact, only when the "natural history" of a disease has been determined in a particular population can effective measures for its control and prevention be devised.[6]

EPIDEMIOLOGICAL RESEARCH IN THE PPSP

Evaluation research has been present from the beginning. It was concerned with the use of the services by those the project was to cover. Studies are being carried out with data from persons registered in the out-patient psychiatric clinics established in El Guabal and Candelaria. In each of these centers, field surveys to measure the mental morbidity—prevalence studies—have been made to gauge the size of the problem and to train the resident in the techniques of field observation.

DATA FROM REGISTERED PATIENTS

In El Guabal the out-patient service for psychiatric patients started on October 1, 1967, after the exploratory period was over, and data is available from that date to June 30, 1969.

The total of 327 patients included 48 adult men, 136 adult women, 78 male patients below 15 years of age, and 65 girls below age 15. Adults totaled 56 per cent and 44 per cent were children.

From previous censuses we know that the sexes are nearly equally represented in El Guabal—49.1 per cent men and 50.9 per cent women in 1964. A field survey in 1968 showed these percentages to be 48.96 for men and 51.04 for women.

Among the psychiatric patients, women outnumbered men 3 to 1, but there was less disparity among the children.

Table 1. Psychiatric Patients Registered in El Guabal at the end of July 1969.

	Men	Women	Total	Percentage
Adults	48	136	184	56
Children	78	65	143	44
Total	126	201	327	100

Several hypotheses might be offered to explain this difference. If we accept the assertion that psychiatric pathology does not affect one sex more frequently than the other, then the fact that more women than men asked for psychiatric treatment might be due to differences in accessibility to the facilities, or to differences between the sexual roles in the adult population.

If there were differences in the accessibility to the psychiatric service, we had to prove that men cannot use the medical programs, which are open from 9 A.M. to 5 P.M., because those are the same hours as those of most jobs in the city. Also, we had to find if the employed men were receiving some kind of psychiatric assistance at their jobs.

This assumption is based on the analysis of occupations of 49 patients who had been seen during the first semester, from October 1, 1967 to March 31, 1968. Of 41 women, 35 were housewives, dressmakers, or unemployed, and only 6 had jobs at factories or as teachers, house servants, or clerks. On the other hand, of 8 male patients, only 2 were unemployed.

The sharp difference in sexual roles could also account for the disparity. It has been reported in Honduras that men use alcohol for alleviating emotional problems.[7] Also, because of the cultural attribute known as *machismo* (courage, pride, manliness), it is expected that men will endure problems without complaining to people other than very close friends, and then usually only when intoxicated. *Machismo* is not demanded of small children and alcohol is not allowed before the age of 15, and we see that in the latter group boys in El Guabal outnumber girls. On the other hand, women are expected not to drink, and it is acceptable for them to complain overtly about difficulties to other women, doctors, priests, or witchdoctors.[8]

These assumptions are valid for most other Latin American countries.[9] In order to prove them in El Guabal, we would have to study alcoholism and other cultural patterns which are not clear at present.

Because of the lack of other studies we cannot dismiss the hypothesis that women in El Guabal, owing to their specific role, are under greater and more frequent stress as a result of unresolved everyday frustrations. Women are dependent on a husband who is absent most of the time—when he does not desert the family—or who spends his money on alcohol. After women reach the same economic status as men through education, the difference observed in El Guabal should disappear.

In rural areas, husband and wife divide economic duties and other responsibilities equally, but when they migrate to the city this balance is disrupted.

In El Guabal, it was found that only 8 per cent of the people registered in psychiatry during the first year had been born in Cali. The rest came from rural areas of southwestern Colombia. On the other hand, most of the children had been born in El Guabal, and both boys and girls went to school. Perhaps this accounts for the more similar figures for children of different sexes coming to the psychiatric service.

In rural Candelaria, 45 patients had been treated from July

1968 to July 1969. Of this total, 22 were adult women, 7 were adult men, and there were 8 boys and 8 girls below age 15. In spite of the smaller figures, the proportions are almost the same for the age and sex groups as in El Guabal.

But in Candelaria, again, of a sample of 162 families studied in 1969, only 12 (8 per cent) were born in the area, the rest coming from other zones. Here, as in El Guabal, only men work in the sugar cane industry, while women stay at home.

In a census in 1969 which covered 5,326 people, it was found that there were 2,763 men (51.8 per cent) and 2,563 women (48.2 per cent). This small difference is explained by the need for young men in the sugar industry.

Candelaria is rural only because of its small groups—there are none with more than 5,500 inhabitants—and because most of its people work in agriculture. On the other hand, El Guabal is urban only because it belongs to a city of almost 1 million who no longer depend on agriculture.

Nevertheless, the rural outskirts of Cali, as well as the slums, are socially and culturally similar—they are halfway between urbanites and peasants. In Candelaria, new agricultural technology demands new skills from the workers, putting them in the same situation as the newcomers in the slum. Consequently, roles and stresses are probably alike for the individuals in both test areas.

The diagnoses of 241 persons registered in the PPSP in El Guabal from October 1, 1967 to Jan. 1, 1969 show that 45 (18.5 per cent) suffer mental retardation, 27 (11 per cent) epilepsy, 20 (8 per cent) schizophrenia, 19 (8 per cent) brain damage, and 12 (5 per cent) effective psychosis. Among the "minor" disorders there are 71 (29.5 per cent) with neurosis, 30 (12 per cent) with personality disturbance, and 5 (2 per cent) with psychophysiological reactions. There are also 11 (5 per cent) patients with other diagnoses, such as temporary adjustment reaction and enuresis. Since these figures reflect the early stages of the program, they cannot be accepted as reliable indicators of the situation in El Guabal as a whole. In this group of 241 patients, 142 were adults and 99 children.

At the end of 1968, there were also 32 persons registered in the PSP who had not been diagnosed. This makes a total of 273 persons registered in the first 18 months (out of a total of 327 in two years, of which 127 were enrolled because they were sent for a psychiatric interview as part of a prevalence study in June 1968. The other group of 256 asked, either by themselves or through their families, for psychiatric care.

In order to know how the patients used the PPSP, two follow-up studies were conducted in the field in May 1968 and in May 1969.

In May 1968, 49 patients who had been enrolled during the first semester were studied through the files of the Medical Center and then at their homes. It was found that 20 had received psychiatric treatment before initiation of the PPSP. Only 6 had been referred by doctors from other medical programs, while 43 came of their own volition or after talking with the assistant nurse who visited the family. Only 5 patients lived in Zone III, the poorest in El Guabal and the farthest from the Parochial Center. Finally, 27 patients had gone once for psychiatric interviews but never returned. On the other hand, 1 patient had 6 and another 7 appointments in six months. A total of 110 interviews were carried out with 49 patients in 6 months.

These data show that the facilities were being underutilized, since 27 patients (57 per cent) did not come back for checkups after the first interview. During the 6 months, there were 288 hours of medical care available for psychiatric patients, of which only 110 (38 per cent) were utilized. The average medical care per patient was 2.26 hours, which is not even half the minimum of 1 interview per month per patient.

Using 10 foreign post-graduate nursing students who accompanied the assistants during their home visits, it was possible in May 1968 to observe some of the patients who had not returned for checkups. Altogether, they approached 20 families, 3 of which rejected them. Each of the remaining 17 families were observed during 3 visits, which resulted in 48 effective and 4 non-effective interviews with patients and relatives. Each family was the object of a group discussion to determine the patient's treatment.

While the work carried out by these nurses contributed to

observing the life style of the patients and their reasons for underutilizing the services available, it must also be noted that the nurses were foreign, having come to Cali for temporary postgraduate training. Through their collaboration with the PPSP, they were able to learn about the goals of the project.

The diagnosis of the patients was as follows: schizophrenia, 5 cases; affective psychosis, 4; epilepsy, 2; mental deficiency, 1; psychoneurosis, 3; and personality disturbances, 2. These patients and their families gave various reasons for rejecting the program. Nine claimed the fee per visit was too high. Two had not gone back since they had improved after one conversation with the psychiatrist, and after having taken the drugs for a few days. Two others rejected the treatment despite family pressure. In 4 cases, the patients' families rejected the treatment. The 17 patients were given new appointments for the following week, but only 8 returned.

The observations made during this follow-up survey gave an idea of the life of psychiatric patients in their community.

Schizophrenic Patients

1) A 56 year-old patient with schizo-affective schizophrenia had a daughter in the psychiatric hospital in the city of Pasto, 200 miles from Cali. The patient suffered from constant anxiety and depression because she thought her daughter was coming from Pasto on foot and woud meet evil men on the way. The patient's husband and sons were tolerant of her illness, but did not take her to the Center because of lack of money.

2) Another schizophrenic woman was dirty, apathetic, on bad terms with her neighbors, and had hypochondriacal complaints. Her home and children were neglected. The husband cooperated and worked to support his family, but the patient did not return to the Center because she was afraid that the drug might have produced unpleasant side-effects.

3) A male patient, head of the household, had been indifferent to his surroundings for several years. He spoke to himself, left the house for several days at a time, and whenever nobody was watchıng, ate all the family's food. The wife and

daughters took care of the house and worked as domestics and factory workers. They had not returned to the Center because the patient had not showed signs of rapid improvement.

Epileptic Patients

1) One married patient with four children suffered from grand mal convulsions every day. In the first interview with the psychiatrist she was given a prescription which she could not buy. The husband built a small hut next to their house, where he kept the patient in dirt and misery. A neighbor threw food to the patient through a window and cleaned the hut superficially once a week. The patient was in a state of complete deterioration. The husband worked all day outside the home, and the children lived with relatives. Prolonged hospitalization was recommended in this case, but was rejected.

2) A 22-year-old patient lived with her mother and accompanied her to the houses where she worked as a servant. The patient's frequent convulsions frightened the housewives, and consequently the mother's jobs didn't last long. The patient had not returned for a checkup because the mother was afraid that the drugs would worsen the illness.

Mental Retardation

The only retarded patient who was followed up was a 15-year-old girl who was aggressive with neighbors. She lived with her mother and a small brother at her grandmother's house. The patient's mother was a beggar, and she used the patient to obtain aid from charitable institutions but rejected any treatment for her. This patient had arrived in the district with her mother a few months earlier, and both left the grandmother's house after the patient was given an injection of Prolixin.

Affective Psychosis

1) A manic-depressive housewife had suffered from depression on two occasions, accompanied by great psychomotor re-

tardation and loss of weight. She had not gone back to the Medical Center because she went to a city hospital for check-ups, and had improved.

2) A patient with involuntary melancholy continued to suffer from anxiety, depression, and insomnia, but did not go to the Medical Center or take drugs because of lack of money.

3) One patient suffered from psychotic depressive reaction and another from involuntionary melancholy. Both had improved and did not return for a checkup because they felt that they did not need further treatment.

Neurosis

1) A housewife with hysterical neurosis of the dissociative type had marital problems and permanent anxiety. She took the drugs irregularly.

2) A depressive-neurotic patient was in a state of advanced pregnancy and had seven children, the oldest of whom was 14. She did not go to the Medical Center because of lack of money, and because she had to take care of the house and children, who were dirty, undernourished and poorly dressed.

From these brief reports it can be assumed that mental illness is more easily tolerated than poverty. If it is accepted that the so-called "culture of poverty," with its associated malnutrition, illiteracy, and bad housing involves different attitudes toward the world and toward time, these people will propably not understand the long-term value of mental health. Also, poverty means apathy towards change, even if it is for the better. In May 1969, another follow-up survey was planned on the 273 patients who had been enrolled in the PPSP from October 1, 1967 to December 31, 1968. Of that total, 191 patients or their relatives were visited by the assistant nurse in El Guabal, so 70 per cent of the patients were followed up.

It was found that 38 patients (20 per cent) had moved from the *barrio*. Two patients had died of somatic disease and 5 were not at home at the time of the appointment. Thus, it was possible to study 146 patients out of 273. This high rate of failure to respond to an appeal for examination forbids any generalizations. Nevertheless, from the observation of 146 patients, some data may be obtained to guide further research.

Of 71 patients (48.6 percent) found to have recovered, 65 were satisfied with the services of the PPSP, and six were receiving psychiatric care from another clinic. Only 10 of the 75 patients (51.4 per cent) who were still moderately to severely ill were on regular treatment at the time of the inquiry. Six patients overtly rejected the invitation to continue their treatment, and 59 discontinued for various reasons. But by this time, Zone III had been incorporated into the PPSP, with 60 persons registered as psychiatric patients. Also, the fee charged for psychiatric interviews was cut from 8 to 5 Colombian pesos (50 to 30 cents [U.S.]) and the fee for children was 3 pesos (20 cents [U.S.]).

However, the basic problem still remained: the community underutilized the psychiatric services.

FIELD SURVEYS

Three field surveys were carried out by the residents, two studies of prevalence and one study of neurotic symptoms.

Prevalence of Mental Disorders in El Guabal

In El Guabal, two residents in preventive medicine and the resident in psychiatry did this survey. The study was designed to collect socio-demographic data of a representative sample of the population and to test the accuracy of an instrument used with the same population to detect manifest psychiatric disorders—i.e., disorders severe enough to be recognized by lay persons. The data collected were intended to be ordered according to the zones of El Guabal.

The study was carried out between May 29 and June 20, 1968. Eight fifth-year medical students filled out socio-demographic questionnaires and applied the psychiatric case-finding instrument to the sample. The procedure can be summed up as follows:

1) Drawing of a stratified sample of 30 per cent of the do-

mestic units (groups of persons living under the same roof). Each domestic unit was considered also as a working unit.

2) Registration of data.

3) Psychiatric examination of cases found in the field.

4) Analysis of the information.

During five days, starting May 29, a pilot test was carried out on 21 domestic units to train the medical students and to adjust the instruments. From June 5 to June 15 the field work was completed and from June 15 to 20 the information was analyzed.

The case-finding instrument was the *Premisas para Diagnosticar Psicosis Manifiesta, Epilepsia y Deficiencia Mental,* which is a list of symptoms found by C. A. Leon to be frequent in the psychiatric histories filed in the San Isidro Psychiatric Hospital. The *Premisas* were used in El Guabal in 1963 on a sample of 10 per cent of the population, and the cases detected by this instrument agreed with the diagnoses made by a psychiatrist. However, the *Premisas* had not been subjected to tests of sensitivity and specificity, so it was not known if all the possible cases from the sample had been sent to the psychiatrist.

The results of this study were:

1) After excluding persons who arrived at El Guabal less than three months before, the sample population covered 520 domestic units—3,775 people—with an average of 7.25 persons per domestic unit.

2) Most of the domestic units were formed by one family.

3) The distribution of the population according to sex was almost equal (men, 49 per cent and women, 51 per cent).

4) Psychotic women outnumbered psychotic men 3 to 1. Mentally retarded men outnumbered mentally retarded women 2 to 1. Epileptics were equally distributed according to sex.

5) Of the sample population, 50 per cent were less than 15 years old, and 70 per cent less than 24. There were no manifest psychoses in those under 15.

6) Of the sample, 71 per cent had lived in El Guabal more than 4 years. In Zone I, 42 per cent of the population had lived there more than 7 years. The average time of residency in the *barrio* was about the same for the three zones—5.9 years in Zone

I; 5 in Zone II, and 5.1 in Zone III. Most of those who gave positive answers to the *Premisas* had been living in the *barrio* more than 6 years.

7) There was no relation between the prevalence of "cases" and the variables of marital status, education, religion, zone of residency, or per capita monthly income (which averaged $10 [U.S.]).

8) The *Premisas* detected 153 "cases," all of which were sent to a psychiatric interview the next day by the medical student involved. But only 94 per cent kept the appointment.

9) The agreement of diagnosis between the psychiatrist, who did not know the result of the *Premisas,* and that of the case-finding instrument, was only 60 per cent. Among the remaining 40 per cent, most of the "cases" were diagnosed as neuroses and personality disorders.

10) The survey received excellent acceptance, with only 15 domestic units out of 520 rejecting the medical students.

Conclusion. The high rate of failure to keep the appointments seems closely related to the underutilization of services found in follow-up studies. People in El Guabal are not sufficiently motivated to consider their mental health as an important matter. On the other hand, it can be assumed that the brevity of this study did not allow the "cases" sufficient opportunity to receive new appointments. The high rate of disagreement between the *Premisas* and the psychiatric examinations points to some defects in the *Premisas.*

Finally, an estimate of the levels of mental morbidity in El Guabal is impossible from this data.

Prevalence of Mental Disorders in Candelaria

This 1969 study used the same case-finding instrument as the 1968 El Guabal study.

Objectives of the Study:

1) Testing the validity of the "method of giving diagnostic premises to an able informer in order to detect manifest psychosis, epilepsy, and mental retardation."

2) Comparison of this method with the psychiatric interview.

3) Estimating the rate of prevalence of mental disorders in

Candelaria and comparing this result with previous surveys by Leon *et al.,* in El Guabal and the rural population of Cerrito.

Methodology:

1) Preparation of the population to get the required co-operation.

2) Study of the map of Candelaria.

3) Preparation of nursing assistant students in the use of the instrument.

4) Pilot survey on a small group to test the feasibility of using the instrument.

5) Application of the instrument to all the families in the population and census.

6) Obtaining of a systematic sample of 23 per cent of the total housing units in the population (approximately 1 out of every 4 houses in every block).

7) Application of the "method of giving diagnostic premises . . ." and a questionnaire for socio-demographic identification to the sample.

8) Appointment for psychiatric interview for all the persons who gave positive answers to the diagnostic premises.

9) Ordering and analysis of data.

Field Work:

1) At the beginning of November 1968, the psychiatrist presented the project to the priest, the mayor and the heads of community councils, teachers, and other influential persons. They were all asked to communicate the project to the people and to help with it.

2) The map of Candelaria was studied and updated with the sanitation supervisor.

3) At the beginning of November 1968, 23 assistant nursing students learned interrogatory techniques. A pilot study was carried out on 7 families.

4) Diagnostic premises and census of the population were applied between November 15 and December 20, 1968.

5) A new assistant nurse applied the premises to a systematic sample in February and March of 1969.

6) Psychiatric interviews were given during March, April, and May 1969.

Description of Instruments:
1) Socio-economic and family questionnaire.
2) Identification and demographic questions.
3) Diagnostic premises applied to an able informer in each family.

Results:

Of 905 families or 5,326 individuals living in the principal village of Candelaria, 35 per cent of the families had one or more individuals with positive answers to the premises. This result corresponds to a census of the village in November 1968 carried out by the assistant nursing students. Then, in February and March 1969, the new assistant interviewed 210 families of the sample of 23 per cent of the village. In 40 per cent of the families, positive answers were given.

During the next 3 months, the psychiatrist expected to interview the 210 families of the sample at the Medical Center, but only 162 families—18 per cent of the total population and 77 per cent of the sample—came to the appointment. In this new group, 63 families gave positive answers.

The 48 families who failed to keep their appointments with the psychiatrist because of reluctance or migration are a factor in the validity of forthcoming analyses. This recalcitrant group might include many whose psychiatric problems make them hesitant to report for an interview. According to Reid, less than 5 per cent is acceptable as a "dropout" rate, but in this study the rate was 18 per cent.

Finally, the psychiatrist had 69 individuals with positive answers to the premises in 63 families of the sample. These families did not differ significantly from the 520 families previously surveyed in the village. After psychiatric interviews of those 69 individuals, 58 were diagnosed as suffering manifest mental disorders.

We now have 58 "manifest cases" in 210 families, or a population of 1,130 individuals. If it were possible to dismiss the 48 families who failed to come for examination, we could estimate a prevalence rate roughly equivalent to 58 per 1,000 population.

This rate was compared with prevalence rates determined by C. A. Leon, using the same case-finding instrument. In El Guabal in 1963, the prevalence of manifest mental disorders was 59.58 per 1,000 population.[10] In the rural village of El Cerrito, near Cali, prevalence was estimated in 1967 at 62.6.[11]

Although the prevalence studies carried out by the residents in the PPSP do not yield definitive findings, they are presented as an aid in research and a guide to the problems a scientist can expect to find when he decides to use the epidemiological approach on populations previously without psychiatric services.

Neuroses in El Guabal

To complete the presentation of research activities conducted by residents, a field study by the resident in charge of the PPSP in El Guabal during the second year of the psychiatric program in the *barrio* will be summed up. Besides the training, this study was to delineate the more frequent symptoms of neurotic illness, described in popular language, in order to design a simple, reliable case-finding instrument for these disorders. The study was conducted on 30 adult patients registered and diagnosed as psychoneurotics in the PPSP. There were 28 women and 2 men, constituting half of the total adult neurotics filed in El Guabal.

Each patient had to be interviewed at home by an assistant nurse and was then sent to the Parochial Center for evaluation by a social worker. Finally, the patient had to see the psychiatrist. Five patients failed to come to the Parochial Center, so the study was limited to 23 women and 2 men, all between the ages of 20 and 59. Five lived in common-law union, 13 were married, 1 was separated, 3 were single, and 3 were widows.

Their diagnoses were: anxiety neurosis, 8; hysterical neurosis, 7 (4 of the dissociative and 3 of the conversive type); depressive neurosis, 7; and hypochondriac neurosis, 3.

These patients had from 11 children to none. Less than 5 children were found in 70 per cent of the families and 30 per cent had from 6 to 11. Most of them owned dwellings given to them by the ICT, and the members of the family numbered from 3 to 12. None of the individuals in the study lived by themselves and all had low incomes.

The most frequent symptoms were different kinds of headaches, like *picada del cerebro* (prick in the back of the head), *puntada en la cabeza* (stitch in the head), *abombamiento de la cabeza* (dilation), or *opresion de la cabeza* (oppression). Next frequent were sensations of peripheral vascular dilation, like *fogaja* (fire), *bochorno* (hot), *olas de calor* (warm waves), and problems of the senses: *fastidio de la vista* (eye nuisances), *zumbidos de oido* (humming), or *nudo en la garganta* (knot in the throat). Backaches and pains in the neck were also frequent. Complaints of weakness or insecurity were expressed in such terms as *tembladera* or *temblesia* (tremor or thrill), *aflojamiento del cuerpo* (loosening of the body), *desmadejamiento* (languishment), and *paralisis del cuerpo* (paralysis).

Pressure and palpitations in the chest and heart were expressed as *asfixia del corazon* (asphyxia of the heart) and *sensacion de ahogo* (choking, suffocation). Patients also felt *borrachera* (drunkenness without alcohol), nausea, vomiting, and *mareo* (sick).

Ataque is a term used both for epileptic seizures and for any acute emotional crisis: *ataque de asfixia* for acute anxiety and *ataque de llanto* for acute distress and depression. *Ida de la cabeza* (the head is gone away) is probably a feeling of depersonalization, the same as *volverse automata* (to become an automaton). Crying, insomnia, and conversion/dissociation were common.

A widespread fear of the future was rationalized through fear of accidents and impending disaster. Impotent rage, without a clear objective, was a repeated complaint. But suicidal thoughts and self-accusation, remorse, or guilt have not been reported in these patients. There seem to be no sexual problems either.

To sum up, the noted somatic expressions of emotional problems could be a reflection of the so-called "culture of poverty."

The complaints of neurotic patients in Candelaria have also been reported. The most frequent symptom was *deseo de salir corriendo* (desire to run away) and *deseo de morirse* (wish to die). Women often reported dissatisfaction with their marital life. As happened with the prevalence studies, these reports cannot be considered definitive findings. However, these sketchy results are a basis for future investigations of similar psycho-social problems and ways of preventing psychiatric diseases and of promoting mental health.

NOTES

1. Jaspers, K., *General Psychopathology*, Chicago, The University of Chicago Press, 1963, p. 5.
2. *Ibid.*, pp. 37–38.
3. WHO, *Technical Report Series*, No. 252, p. 32.
4. *Ibid.*, p. 30.
5. *Ibid.*, No. 185, p. 3.
6. *Ibid.*, pp. 5–6.
7. Hudgens, R. W., *et al.*, *Psychiatric Illness.* . . .
8. Kiev, *Curanderismo.*
9. Reid, D. D., *Epidemiological Methods in the Study of Mental Disorders*, WHO, 1960, p. 61.
10. Leon, C. A., *Prevalencia de Trastornos Mentales en un Sector Urbano de Cali*, VI Congreso Colombiano de Psiquiatria, Pasto, 1966.
11. Leon, C. A. et al., *Evaluacion de Instrumentos pare el Estudio de la Prevalencia de Trastornos Mentales*, V Congreso APAL, Bogotá, 1968.

BIBLIOGRAPHY ON EL GUABAL AND CANDELARIA

Argandona, M., *Psiquiatria Social, Un Ano de Actividades en El Guabal*, Cali, Departamento de Psiquiatria, Universidad del Valle, 1968 (typescript).

Gil, Villanueva, and Argandona, M., *Estudio de Prevalencia de Trastornos Mentales Manifiestos en el Barrio El Guabal*, Cali, Departamento de Psiquiatria, Universidad del Valle, 1968 (typescript).

Jimenez, V., *Centro Parroquial San Juan Bautista, Barria El Guabal*, Cali, Departamento de Medicina Preventiva y Salud Publica, U. V., 1967 (mimeograph).

Lourido, E., *Prevalencia de Trastornos Mentales en la Poblacion de Candelaria*, Cali, Departamento de Psiquiatria, Universidad del Valle, 1969 (typescript).

Lourido, E., *Psiquiatria Social, Un Ano de Actividades en Candelaria*, Cali, Departamento de Psiquiatria, Universidad del Valle, 1969 (typescript).

Matute, G., *Psiquiatria Social: Segundo Ano de Actividades en El Guabal*, Cali, Departamento de Psiquiatria, Universidad del Valle, 1969 (typescript).

PART THREE

The PPSP and Latin America

CHAPTER 14

Assessment

ANTECEDENTS

THE new mental health programs developed in Cali by the Universidad del Valle, under the name of Pilot Plan of Social Psychiatry, offer an unprecedented opportunity for Latin American psychiatry to upgrade its capacity to take care of developing societies. These societies experience the stresses of change and frustration as they awaken after centuries of apathetic indifference.

If the PPSP is able to take advantage of what is now known regarding the prevention of psychiatric problems, the newborn social psychiatry program might lead to substantial improvement in the health of Latin Americans, health meaning, as WHO has defined it, ". . . complete physical, mental and social well-being and not merely the absence of disease or infirmity."[1]

Specifically, it is expected that the PPSP will prevent mental illness at the three levels within the population covered by its functions. Two years of experience have shown considerable opportunities for such prevention.

However, it has become clear over those two years that the simple organization of a comprehensive psychiatric service ranging from the education of the public through hospitalization for the most seriously ill does not in itself ensure the best utilization of opportunities, neither by the public nor by psychiatrists. Undoubtedly, the PPSP has increased the probability of early and adequate treatment and the opportunity for psychiatrists to learn more about the individuals and families under his care and to make use of new approaches to develop his potential as scientific researcher and health leader of the community.

When the PPSP was initiated, it was made responsible for the psychiatric problems of the people in El Guabal and Candelaria, and its purpose was to carry out preventive, educational, orgaanizational, and research activities. At the time it was said that, ". . . the experiences of public health have demonstrated that community-oriented programs yielded a notable progress in the control of several disorders even before knowing their specific etiology, . . ." and that ". . . although our knowledge in the field of psychiatry is incomplete, we have sufficient information to diminish the magnitude of mental disease." Also, the Department of Psychiatry of the Universidad del Valle had considered it ". . . crucial to give its post-graduate trainees the opportunity to develop social psychiatry activities. During the last year of his training, the resident has enough experience to carry out important tasks in the community."[2]

The hypothesis was stated as: Mental illness can be not only better handled, but also diminished by the social approach to psychiatry, with focus on environmental, anthropological, and economic factors influencing the local community, rather than on the sporadic attention of isolated patients.

FIELD WORK

In July 1967 one resident went to El Guabal and another to Candelaria. They were financed with the help of ICAMI and supervised by the Department of Psychiatry. It was not necessary to provide more staff directly in the field because one of the objectives of the PPSP was to create new functions based on personnel and facilities already involved in public health.

Thus, a remarkable feature of the PPSP is its economy in a situation lacking both abundant funds and manpower. The resident spent two months acquainting himself with the community and the Public Health Center. This exploratory period served to make the public and the public health workers receptive and motivated to cooperate with the new program and the new staff member.

As was predicted, the number of people asking for help after the program opened kept increasing. An estimated 350 people in El Guabal were suffering mental disorders at the end of 1966, and by the middle of 1969, 327 people had been registered in the PPSP. It can be predicted that these figures will increase slowly until they reach a point of saturation, after which the increase will follow the population growth rate. The number of patients registered during the first year of activities was almost the same in El Guabal (49) as in Candelaria (45).

Also, the number of psychiatric interviews and home visits increased consistently during the first two years of the PPSP as these activities became the responsibility of medical students and assistant nurses.

However, most of the patients—especially those who needed more attention—failed to keep on with their treatment, therefore hampering the preventive activities of the PPSP. Two field studies showed that the underutilization of services is a complex sociocultural problem demanding a multidisciplinary approach to motivate an apathetic community.

Regarding educational activities, it has been shown how different levels of training were achieved and how education involved many people, both as trainers and trainees. During the first year, almost all of the educational activities were the responsibility of the resident, but during the second year, the medical students and assistant nurses were able to give information and assistance to different groups in El Guabal. Furthermore, social workers, teachers, priests, and policemen were cooperating actively as channels of communication, while the resident acted as a coordinator and consultant in psychiatric problems. By now it should be possible to expand educational activities to include the study and diffusion of specific preventive techniques at any of the three preventive levels (for instance, by trying the find and correct cultural habits which could interfere with sound adaptation to school or job, or by seeking factors which operate on the "deprivation syndrome"). Again, this suggestion involves a multidisciplinary approach, including epidemiology and the social sciences.

Organizational activities can be called leadership activities. Little is known about what makes a leader. Research in this area will lead to progress in other aspects of organization, such as administration, cost accounting, and raising funds for mental health.

In El Guabal and Candelaria, the resident was able to organize a congenial team and to distribute functions among the personnel of the health centers and also among some significant members of the community. Thanks to such organization, activities and coverage were expanded in other areas, i.e., education, prevention, and research.

The PPSP gave the residents their first opportunity to do independent research. Although they were supervised, it would be unrealistic to expect accurate results from this kind of research. Although it was not possible to obtain definitive rates of prevalence and incidence of mental disorders in the population, most of the data presented in this work come from the exact observations and measures by the residents of several variables in the population, such as age, housing, and incomes. Also, the PPSP studied people who are not similar, socially or culturally, to the researchers. Thus, only tentative conclusions can be reached which will pave the way for future investigation and preventive experiments in the community.

The working hypothesis of the PPSP cannot be rejected; mental illness is being better handled. But we still do not know if mental illness is really diminishing in El Guabal and Candelaria. Furthermore, the stress on environmental, anthropological, social, and economic factors must be increased to get a comprehensive approach to the problem of mental health and a better understanding of present obstacles to PPSP. Technical assistance from experts in sciences other than psychiatry might be called for, but it is probably more important first to emphasize the social sciences. However, psychiatric problems in El Guabal and Candelaria have been greatly ameliorated at very low cost and with minimal disruption of ways of living. Immediate assistance in crisis, the avoidance of undesirable labeling of patients, the possibility of taking care of most of the problems within the family, are, among others, all important advancements in mental health for the community as a whole.

NOTES

1. U.N., WHO, "Constitution of the WHO."
2. Departamento de Psiquiatria, *Plan Piloto* . . . , Universidad del Valle, Cali, 1967.

CHAPTER 15

Practicability

LATIN AMERICA'S CRISIS

COULD the PPSP be useful in other Latin American cities and rural areas? This question can only be answered by launching and later evaluating similar plans in other areas.

For the present, we can consider the needs and resources of the Latin American countries and consider the application of the PPSP or an alternative approach to the problem of mental health in the region as a whole. As has been explained, Latin America cannot be thought of as a homogeneous underdeveloped region. Instead, it consists of a heterogeneous group of nations sharing some common problems and working together to solve them according to local conditions.

However, similar problems have been described among all the Latin American countries. Even in the more developed of the 20 nations, there are problems of population and poverty, rapid unplanned urbanization, unemployment, illiteracy, and violence. There is a high level of frustration and maladjustment evidenced by disintegrated families, crime, alcoholism, and prostitution. Distress and disorientation, as frequent as the resistance to cooperate with local or national planning, is expressed in passive apathy or explosive aggression.

On the other hand, everyone is convinced that the spectacular achievements of technology, science, and industry will raise the standards of living, and that, eventually, all Latin Americans will participate in the benefits of progress and development. Consequently, Latin America as a region faces a "crisis in expectations"[1] in that the people find it difficult to adjust to learning new skills or to taking new risks. This increases frustration and makes keener the contrast between theirs' and the more privileged ways of life. Under this pressure, radical solutions that further increase individual tensions and bar collective progress are sought.

How useful could a program like the PPSP be in Latin America?

PSYCHIATRIC HELP

To orient the individual to the changes produced by progress, to alleviate the anxieties about new challenges, and to avoid the frustrations that build up as tradition breaks down, the psychiatrist already has efficient techniques. He can show how to discharge the everyday tensions in constructive ways and make it easier to accept new ideas and to abandon now-useless defensive mechanisms. Technical change is blamed for increasing mental illness, but psychological insight is the best preventive measure in this dilemma.

As has been written in a UNESCO publication.

Technical change disrupts old habits. What has the psychiatrist to say about the effects within the individual personality of such a disruption? Technical change makes it difficult for individuals to pattern their lives as adults on the lives which, as children, they watched their parents live. What can psychiatry say about the loss of parental models, or the conflicts involved in trying both to keep and to break away from parental models of behavior? Technical change involves new learning, after adulthood, and changing types of behavior which have been heavily reinforced by childhood experiences of reward and punishment. What can psychiatry say of the type of anxiety, conflict and healthy stimulus which a challenge to new learning provides?[2]

THE EXAMPLE OF PPSP

The PPSP tries to answer these questions and to find ways of preventing the psychic consequences of the suddenness and unfamiliarity of progress.

We have seen in El Guabal and Candelaria the conflicts and psychiatric symptoms accompanying technical change and urbanization; we saw how these conflicts are expressed and how they disrupt the family and individual lives. It seems that women and children are most sensitive to these stresses, or at least they are the ones who seek help at the beginning. This predominance of women and children increases the potential of psychiatric techniques, for an adult woman maintains a central position in the home where she spends most of her time. By treating relatively unformed children we can better utilize preventive psychiatry.

We have also seen that in El Guabal and Candelaria the pressures of change, mental stress, and illness are dynamic and versatile entities which change as much as the environment and the individuals. A continuum is apparent, moving between health and illness, sometimes slowly, sometimes very quickly, following the pressures of environmental and individual changes. Relatively, we cannot admit as symptoms of disease the usual frustration and discomfort caused by the social change itself. But we have to treat the crises that arise as consequences of that frustration and discomfort after a trivial event acted as the last straw. According to the criteria of "crises intervention,"[3] the attention given to these situations has always been immediate and intensive in El Guabal: the psychiatric personnel visited the patient at home, daily if necessary, to give emotional support, psychopharmacological medicines, and social guidance. When one person and his family was considered in psychiatric emergency, they received top priority care. With this approach it was relatively easy to treat the illnesses.

Apathy, resistance, and chronic complaints made it more difficult to carry out preventive techniques in some cases; nevertheless, a number of patients in El Guabal eventually accepted the PPSP, thus avoiding hospitalization or increasing complications of their problems. During the second year of the PPSP in El Guabal, this acceptance was easier thanks to the collaboration of other agents of the community when the family was not cooperative.

These activities are being developed by the PPSP in spite of the scarcity of personnel and funds. The most feasible aspects of the PPSP for use anywhere in Latin America are:

1) The psychiatrist goes into the community rather than waiting for patients to take the initiative.

2) Within the community, the psychiatrist observes and studies all the events likely to be related to psychiatry, whether social or individual.

3) After he is well informed about the local community, he assesses psychiatric needs and looks for local resources to aid his program.

4) The utilization of local resources has been exemplified in the PPSP by the use of medical centers and the training of public health personnel, thus avoiding initial expenses.

5) After starting the public activities, the principal function of the psychiatrist is that of leadership in order to coordinate the teamwork and to reach the whole community.

6) If the psychiatrist becomes accepted as a leader it will be easier to expand his program and to initiate scientific research.

7) Activities increase in range and complexity, and more people are involved in preventive psychiatry, as happened in El Guabal during the second year, although new difficulties may appear, especially the underutilization of services and facilities.

8) At this point leadership must motivate the the population to better utilize the psychiatric services as well as to introduce new patterns of behavior into traditional ways of life. From this point on, it will be necessary to use the knowledge and techniques of the social sciences, especially cultural anthropology, sociology, epidemiology, and public administration, as well as psychiatry.

9) From the beginning of the PPSP, accurate filing and regis

tration of each patient allowed rapid censuses and follow-up studies. However, registration and filing systems should have enough flexibility to allow improvements in data gathered for research and for comparison.

10) Evaluation of the preventive and therapeutic effectiveness of psychiatric services like the PPSP must be made to allow their broader application. Such research must be carried out at intervals and should take into account changes in the management and treatment of patients. In the Department of Psychiatry in Cali, seminars were held to report the progress of the PPSP at the end of each semester of activities in El Guabal and Candelaria. During the seminar the resident presented the results of his work and then discussed with the staff of the Department of Psychiatry both the difficulties he had met and possibilities for the next semester.

So far, we have presented the results of the first to the fourth semesters of activities carried out in Cali by the PPSP.

The above-mentioned aspects show that the originality of the PPSP lies in its emphasis on an active approach to local problems, thus departing from the traditional image of a patient on a couch or in a hospital ward being attended by a specialist who does not consider problems other than the symptoms or the buried past of his patient.

Because the PPSP means an active, economical encounter with the social environment, we believe that it is a feasible model for use in other areas of Latin America, and that as a demonstration project it could be accepted as a substitute for "experience." Psychiatrists could, therefore, learn in a few weeks the facts about the PPSP,[4] since it was planned and developed by local psychiatrists with a background similar to that of most Latin American psychiatrists, and was carried out in an environment similar to others in the subcontinent. Finally, not only native residents in psychiatry, but graduate doctors and graduate nurses from different Latin American countries, worked in the two test areas.[4a]

NOTES

1. *The Rockefeller Report* . . . , p. 19.
2. Mead (Ed.), *op. cit.*, p. 269.

3. Parad, H. J. (Ed.), *Crisis Intervention: Selected Readings,* New York, Family Service Association of America, 1965.

4. Mead (Ed.), *op. cit.,* p. 302.

4a. Besides two residents who were born in Cali during the two years described, three other residents worked in the PPSP: one from Cartagena, Colombia, one from Bolivia, and one from Ecuador. Also, residents from Brazil and Peru in the Department of Preventive Medicine of the Universidad del Valle cooperated with the PPSP during this initial two-year period.

CHAPTER 16

Optional Models

THE PPSP AS A NATIONAL PLAN

THE feasibility of the PPSP as a pilot for other Latin American cities has been demonstrated. However, a slum or rural village cannot be accepted as a perfect model for a city or nation, so the project must be modified for a different and larger situation.

Although the PPSP is being developed in Colombia, that nation's particular features have to be considered in comparison with other countries where the PPSP could be emulated. Furthermore, the PPSP is a product of a university which has been community-oriented for longer than a decade, within a city which has had one of the highest ratios of economic and population growth in Latin America during the period after World War II.

According to Lambert, Colombia—along with Brazil, Venezuela and Mexico—exemplifies countries "in which rapid economic development is proceeding and bringing about far-reaching social changes."[1] These nations have been described by Lambert as "developing countries." On the other hand, he describes Uruguay and

Argentina as "post-development" countries because their development is already well advanced, although proceeding slowly over the last few years, and points out "pre-development" countries with a very low and slowly rising per capita income, literacy rate, and the like. Therefore, Colombia holds the middle position in terms of development, and its situation and programs can better be compared with those of similar countries.

Since 1967, there has been a National Plan of Mental Health in Colombia, projected until 1977,[2] the largest program of mental health attempted so far which would cover the whole nation. The plan recommends, among other things, creating mental health centers, promoting the teaching of mental health principles, developing research, and orienting psychiatric services toward the community.

The PPSP fits this national plan, which could be another reason to account for its early progress.

LOCAL ACTION

It has been seen that, in countries like Mexico and Colombia, the central government is aware of the significance of mental health and is active in pursuing it.

Local acceptance, however, is more important than official recognition. To a considerable extent, the success of any effort of social change depends on popular motivation. Substantial improvement in mental health could be achieved if local populations would follow changes in habits proposed by the psychiatrist which do not require particular education or expense.[3]

As has been pointed out, people in both El Guabal and Candelaria were already motivated to accept public health measures, and they were used to cooperating with research activities after several years of profiting from the work of the Department of Preventive Medicine of the Universidad del Valle, which produced quick and effective benefits. As a corollary, the PPSP, a simple, practical, and inexpensive project, had its success assured almost before its beginning.

The Department of Psychiatry of the Universidad del Valle has a staff of psychiatrists who were oriented toward social problems long before the beginning of PPSP. Under the direction of C. A. Leon, they were studying the entire population of Cali and nearby areas until they chose the opportunity of introducing a new and effective program in social psychiatry. They avoided conflicts with local or national authorities and agencies by directing their activities to a field free from overt competition which was ready to accept the proposed innovations. This approach illustrates the importance of pioneering in development without relying on paternalistic support.

Other characteristics that maximized the chances of success of the PPSP were its stress on practical and safe techniques such as the use of tranquilizers, anti-convulsants, and other medicines, as well as the abolition of waiting lists, the urgent crisis intervention, supportive psychotherapy and, in a wider sense, the use of public health concepts and strategy. It is also important to emphasize that the PPSP started in areas where the need for psychiatric services already existed as the consequence of several years of preventive work in medical problems: people who had their physical health needs taken care of became aware of emotional difficulties.

Finally, the PPSP focused on a concentrated attack on a "bottleneck" with a paucity of resources. It was a selective approach to a problem limited both geographically and in terms of variety of services. It means that the PPSP did not intend to cover the whole city of Cali, nor the Departamento del Valle, just as it did not intend to offer all possible psychiatric facilities and services.

In the long run, the PPSP could be called a catalytic agent in articulating and providing a means for channeling the Latin American desire for better mental health.

ALTERNATIVE APPROACHES

A comprehensive plan of social psychiatry might be desirable when a beginning has to be made almost from scratch and many interacting concerns require attention. The comprehensive approach can give a "thin spread" effect on which broad-based foundations for further selective or specific growth could be based (the pyramid idea); also, this approach could meet the broad demands of all segments of the population. Most of the national plans launched by the central government are on this order and should especially be considered in countries with a steady central authority in the midst of a "predeveloped society" (in the sense given to this expression by Lambert), where it is likely that social psychiatry is already an unknown quantity. However, the choice of the concentrated, selective approach has to be borne constantly in mind, primarily because of the limited resources, many needs, and the desirability of showing quick benefits to catch people's attention and cooperation.

This option leads to another possibility, which is the choice of government action instead of waiting for the initiative of private individuals. This approach has to be contemplated especially when there is a lack of expert personnel and of technical organization. This plan would give the central government an idea of the social and psychological stresses caused by technological change, so it can institute preventive measures in the disturbing process of rapid economic development so that:

> . . . proper measures can be taken to ensure that economic changes do not in fact create social distress . . . that socially pathological conditions, such as delinquency and narcotic addiction, do not undermine the population. . . . No program of technological development can hope to succeed in the long run if it leaves people unhappy and maladjusted.
> . . .This is not a necessary consequence of technological development, but it is a possible one.[5]

However, mental health is not of high priority in Latin America. Jones has pointed that out:

> It seems likely that those who administer the mental health services will always have difficulty in securing the share of national resources which social justice demands. The proper care of psychiatric patients costs a good deal of money, and it is difficult to demonstrate an adequate return of investments. A proportion of mental health work is, and perhaps always must be, economically unproductive.[6]

These facts are compounded by political authorities who are satisfied with a shallow and perfunctory approach to these problems. There is also an irrational opposition even to accept the existence of the problem of mental illness, which is presumably based on the uncanny fear which mental illness inspires in the lay population. Therefore, psychiatrists and mental health professionals have to be responsible for advocating the implementation of proper psychiatric programs.

PREREQUISITES

As has been seen in the second part of this book, the PPSP started in El Guabal and Candelaria after desirable social pre-conditions were achieved. Obviously, these pre-conditions paved the way for the PPSP by fulfilling existing needs. However, in areas where local needs cannot be fulfilled immediately, it is suggested that methods be developed for communicating knowledge and information concerning new practices, bearing in mind that compulsory education or health measures have to be introduced when the local population is ignorant of its needs. This awakening of awareness means to create new needs, which are the responsibility of the professional in providing relevant information. The problem of raising new needs has to be studied carefully. The desire for innovation in the field of mental health could merely stimulate a desire for consumption, which would eventually lead to a frustration if the means were inadequate.

Mental health promoters could use the mass media, which have proved effective in creating a receptivity to innovation, although it is not so effective in initiating any real action.

The skillful handling of local leaders is another key factor for the successful introduction of social projects. Here the first requirement should be careful identification and selection of local leaders, and next their training.

Varying background factors may explain reluctance to adopt changes. Dire poverty, low level of health, traditional fatalism and apathy are among the general problems which create hesitation on the part of those living on the edge of subsistence to take certain risks of innovation without some guarantee against failure.

In rural areas the land tenure system may discourage those who work the land, if the benefits go to others.

Suspicion of government, or excessive dependency on it, as well as conflict between the proposed changes and cultural or religious values, will hamper open communication. Isolation or illiteracy may make it difficult even to understand the proposition of change, especially if it is presented in unfamiliar concepts.

The lack of adequate administrative machinery, or the dependency of a proposed change on an institutional framework (for example, the dependency of health innovation, such as the use of new machines, on a complex of technical, informational, and credit services) will paralyze a program even after some positive steps. have been taken.[7]

By and large, the effects of improving the level of living indirectly help to remove obstacles and to build up attitudes favorable to development. Psychiatrists, as experts in communication and social interaction, are in a strategic position to support and orient motivation campaigns, not only within the field of mental health, but also in such areas as public health, education, family planning, and others that will eventually raise the mental health of the population and will lay the groundwork for more specific programs.

In conclusion, the primary objectives of social psychiatry should be to increase to a maximum the achievements of existing facilities and manpower, and to coordinate social services, in order to make it easier to apply more specific psychiatric projects. This indirect approach should be emphasized, especially in countries where psychiatry is not customarily utilized by the people, who so far could be unaware of their mental health problems, or are even reluctant to begin a change proposed by the professionals. In such a situation, research will produce more results if it is incorporated in programs which cover other demands, such as education or health.

Psychiatrists must also be the educators and promoters of mental health outside clinical services, and they should be required, also, to cooperate with international agencies in approaching the common problems of underdevelopment and social change.

NOTES

1. Lambert, J., "Requirements for Rapid Economic and Social Development" in E. De Vries and J. Medina Echavarria, *Social Aspects of Economic Development in Latin America*, UNESCO, 1963, p. 52.

2. *Informe Sobre la Salud Mental en Colombia*, V Congreso APAL, Bogotá, 1968.

3. A general discussion on popular motivation can be found in: U.N., *1965 World Social Situation*.

4. The theme "Comprehensiveness versus Selectivity" is presented in: U.N., *1965 World Social Situation*, pp. 9–10.

5. Mead (Ed.), *op. cit.*, pp. 309–27.

6. Jones, K., *British Experience in Community Care*, in Henry P. David (Ed.), *op. cit.*, p. 91.

7. U.N., *1965 World Social Situation*, p. 5.

CHAPTER 17

Looking at the Future

THE NEED FOR EXPANSION

THE PPSP is still young and growing. Its achievements cannot be accurately measured, but the number of patients it covers is steadily increasing. Doctors are acquiring new skills to better understand and help their communities. Apathy is being gradually replaced by hope and motivation for health improvement.

By 1969, almost 50,000 people had been reached by the PPSP. However, the influence of the program extends beyond these figures. Young doctors and nurses trained in El Guabal and Candelaria are already making available—to their patients elsewhere—mental health techniques which are adaptable to their own situation. Perhaps most important for the PPSP's near future is its need for expansion in many directions. Basic areas will be pointed out which are particularly susceptible to change and evolution, whether in response to local and regional pressures or according to a careful plan. These basic areas are education, research, therapy, and organization.

EDUCATION

Regarding education, it has been shown how the PPSP teaches social psychiatry within a community, thus giving psychiatrists and allied personnel the opportunity to appreciate the collective needs of the people, and to assess their own capacity to fulfill those needs. A psychiatrist working in the PPSP also appreciates the importance of teamwork and learns how to train the personnel needed to deal with community problems.

However, the resident in psychiatry receives little or no instruction in the art of teaching. Medical faculties should provide opportunities at least for self-education in this role.[1]

In El Guabal and Candelaria, the postgraduate is responsible for tutoring and training undergraduates and nurses. His principal exercise as future teacher is the "feedback" from the trainees, which helps him evaluate the effectiveness of his teaching. The postgraduate also acquires familiarity with varied techniques of teaching by participating in and conducting interviews, courses, and discussion groups with the community and his team. Psychiatrists can instruct clergymen, nurses, schoolteachers, policemen, lawyers, and others in the prevention and management of minor psychiatric crises in everyday life. Since there are few established precedents for these types of teaching, it is particularly important to observe carefully what is being done in the PPSP and to take full advantage of the potential implications of the PPSP as a program to provide specific training in the art of teaching psychiatry, which is a prerequisite to extend psychiatric practice into preventive work. So far, most of the training programs for psychiatrists stress the need for a broad, humanistic training in psychiatry.[2] Although the necessity of community organization and a social approach had frequently been mentioned in a Latin American seminar on the subject of teaching of psychiatry held in Lima in December 1967,[3] there was no clear conception about the methods and strategy needed to tackle this challenging situation.

In the PPSP, psychiatrists and undergraduates get some awareness of the significance of social factors in the cause and treatment
of mental illnesses. However, there is not yet a systematized teaching program in social subjects such as group psychology, sociome-
try, medical sociology, or the basic principles of social and cultural
anthropology.

The importance of social sciences cannot be overestimated,
particularly in connection with the teaching of mental health promotion.[4] Postgraduates and undergraduates must learn that illness
is not only a personal, but also a social condition, and to observe
the patient within the framework of the interpersonal relationships
with family and society.

In a practical way, these methods are being taught and studied
in El Guabal and Candelaria. The systematization and further expansion of training in the social sciences and methods will probably demand the cooperation of a multidisciplinary team which is
not as yet available. Nevertheless, Cali is today one of the few
centers which offers a practical and intensive involvement with
social factors influencing mental health. Consequently, postgraduate students in psychiatry should consider Kiev's advice that Latin
American psychiatrists should train in Cali instead of in the United
States.[5] Besides the advantage of receiving a new and highly so-
phisticated training, the trainee will find he has developed effective
weapons against social and economic underdevelopment in his
country.

This suggestion constitutes a challenge to the trainees, as well
as to the host and the "sending" country. Furthermore, the con-
nections between the Department of Psychiatry of the Universidad
del Valle and a number of international institutions could help to
further increase progress, offering widespread experience for psychiatrists from both developing and developed countries.

The PPSP, as a regional training center for Latin America,
could also help control the "brain drain."[5a] This role has already
been signaled by the fact that two psychiatrists who received their
postgraduate training in Cali did go back to their native countries
and two more still in training are planning to return.

RESEARCH

Research based on international cooperation is necessitated by the multiple and complex problems caused by poverty and disorganization of local resources. Because resources are limited, and everything cannot be done simultaneously, it is necessary to assess carefully the correct ordering of priorities and to evaluate the results of research.[6] This could probably be done more accurately under the supervision of foreign experts who are in a position to make objective judgments of the local situation. This recommendation should be applied when possible, not only to the PPSP, but to all the research projects scheduled for developing countries, especially since the conduct of research programs in several areas might involve large groups of workers, much preparatory activity, and perhaps expensive facilities or laboratories. Much research has to be encouraged, especially since the promotion of mental health and the prevention of mental disorders is a slow process because the problem is so complex.[7]

Although an exact list of priorities is not possible, research should be undertaken according to the local necessities and resources. In Cali, research might be aimed at problems of social change and urbanization which are supposed to influence the population's mental health. Studies on brain function are particularly difficult because of the need for scientists trained in neurochemistry and neurophysiology. However, malnutrition and infectious diseases among the young necessitate this kind of research, as well as genetics studies, particularly in view of the numerous children who fail in school, ostensibly to hypothetical brain deficiency.[8] Research on mental subnormality should include organization of adequate services and educational facilities.[9]

Epidemiological research is certainly the most urgent. At present, only tentative estimates show the distribution of mental disorders. The difficulties of epidemiological research are not yet quite understood. Uncertainties about the definition of a "case" and about heterogeneous populations have been formidable obstacles to the PPSP. There is an urgent need for better ways of approaching field studies within marginal urban and rural communities which are often almost inaccessible. It is also necessary to develop accurate and rapid systems of registration and filing of psychiatric data which eventually would be computer-processed as the basis for international comparisons.

Studies of the impact of promotional programs are inconclusive. Research is needed on how technical change, literacy, parental attitudes, or diet and pharmaceuticals mold the personality and help sound adjustment in different cultures. While working toward better methodology, education in sound mental hygiene should be continued. Research on child development and child rearing are needed but they require much time and money.

In addition, the ecology of mental illness must be studied. Studies at community level reveal the natural history of mental diseases and patterns of deviant behavior in respect to their course and outcome in particular environments. It is to be hoped that techniques and experience will be developed to obtain comparable data for people of different ecological backgrounds in several social, cultural, and climatic areas.

Latin American psychiatrists have paid considerable attention to research oriented to therapy. Clinical trials or evaluation of the effectiveness of different therapeutic methods have been undertaken in several countries. According to WHO, these must clarify two main points: 1) What are the essential features of the treatment program, and what parts can be dropped without impairing its therapeutic efficacy? 2) What is the *minimum* education and training necessary for each of the persons who will carry out the treatments?[10] These two questions lead to experiments that seem feasible within the PPSP.

THERAPY AND PREVENTION OF ILLNESS

The PPSP needs to expand its current therapeutic services in order to cover the three proposed levels of prevention. During its first two years, the bulk of therapeutic activities has been directed toward those persons who have some recognizable psychiatric symptoms, while primary prevention—i.e., promotion of mental health and protection from specific conditions—and tertiary prevention, or rehabilitation of chronic patients, have been partially neglected.

Thanks to the recent achievements of chemotherapy and psychotherapy, it is now relatively easy to treat and cure many patients. By these means secondary prevention is also highly effective, so that benefits can appear quickly and demonstrably. These benefits also have a dramatic quality, encouraging further innovations.

The effects of primary prevention are not so easy to demonstrate as those of secondary prevention, especially because mental health promotion and alleviation of predisposing conditions require slow and gradual recognition and improvement. Only when people have seen immediate and dramatic recoveries from mental disorders will they accept the needed environmental changes.

Rehabilitation of chronic and incurable patients requires complex facilities such as occupational therapy and controlled environments such as farms and day or night hospitals to stop further deterioration in their conditions and to help them become productive members of their community. At this level, it is also necessary to "rehabilitate" the society in order to make it possible for persons traditionally viewed as hopeless, dangerous, or repulsive, to be accepted.

ORGANIZATION

The future of the PPSP depends on organization and administration. As the PPSP expands, it will be necessary to research costs of services with the help of management consultants. Also, it is necessary to decide whether the mental health program should be an independent agency or a division of some other larger agency of the central government.[11] It also must be decided whether educational and research activities on the one hand, and curative and preventive services on the other, should be combined in one agency. So far little is known about the relative value of different organizational patterns or the qualities that make for the needed leadership.

Organization should emphasize projects that provide sustained and continuous employment, especially in localities like Colombian *barrios* and rural villages with a heavy population growth and much unemployment.

According to latest estimates, Colombia will double its population in 22 years,[12] and sooner in urban areas. On the other hand, the teaching potential of medical schools cannot be increased to produce enough doctors to keep up with the population growth. This situation will be compounded by the tendency of doctors to concentrate in the richer urban areas of the principal cities in Colombia. Consequently, in the next decade or two, psychiatric needs in marginal urban areas and the countryside will increase steadily, while the resources of the city and the trained manpower may be at a standstill. The PPSP offers an organizational model which could be used to alter this pessimistic forecast. By training subsidiary personnel, large groups of people can be cared for without excessive expense or numerous highly trained specialists. The organization of existing urban and rural medical centers to take care of urgent psychiatric problems would be a big step forward in the quest for better mental health for Colombia and Latin America. Then the expansion of these services to employ the very people of the community they serve could be considered.

Most Latin American nations would find the PPSP applicable to their own conditions, adapting the plan, when necessary, to local resources and needs.

NOTES

1. WHO, *Technical Report Series,* No. 252, pp. 30–39.
2. "Seminario sobre la Ensenanza de la Psiquiatria y la Salud Mental en las Escuelas de Medicina," *Educacion Medica y Salud,* abril–junio, 1968.
3. *Ibid.*
4. WHO, *Technical Report Series,* No. 252, pp. 11–18.
5. Kiev, A., *La Psiquiatria Social en Colombia,* V Congreso APAL, Bogotá, 1968.
5a. See Chapter 5 under the heading "The University."
6. WHO, *Technical Report Series,* No. 252, pp. 36–39.
7. *Ibid.,* No. 223, pp. 11–12 and 38–54.
8. *Ibid.,* No. 346.
9. *Ibid.,* No. 75.
10. *Ibid.,* No. 223, pp. 46–47.
11. *Ibid.,* p. 47.
12. Sociedad Colombiana de Psiquiatria, *op. cit.*

Epilogue

THE serious social dislocation produced by urban expansion, population explosion, and rejection of traditional ways of life in Latin America has affected individuals of all ages, but especially youth. Along with these problems are the chronic poverty and scarcity of skills to alleviate it. It is a paradox that ample knowledge and technological resources exist today to achieve dramatic improvements in living conditions in developing countries. For example, the knowledge exists to wipe out much of the world's malnutrition and disease, and to produce much more food. Yet this knowledge is not applied.[1]

Part of the explanation of the paradox lies in the fact that perhaps too much hope has been placed in political leaders, economics, and technicians without considering psychological and social factors which hinder the desired advancement. It is not yet understood that existing psychological and social conditions are as important as the specific activities of science and industry for economic development. It is essential that proper measures be taken to ensure that economic and political changes do not create human distress, that pathological conditions such as psychiatric disorders, delinquency, alcoholism, and narcotic addiction do not undermine the young. Too often the introduction of new techniques and projects has been undertaken without consideration for the effects of such innovations on mental health and social organization. Changes which loosen family ties and alter the patterns of acquisition of status and prestige affect personality development, security, and contentment. Since all social change occurs through the actions of individuals, the task of psychiatrists, psychologists, and social scientists to devise ways of reducing ill effects on individuals who must live within a changing environment and to study traditional habits which could promote or jeopardize the mental health of individuals.[2]

Psychiatric care and psychotherapy could bridge the gap between tradition and change on one hand, and individual adaptive or disruptive response to such conflict on the other.

Accordingly, the significance of social psychiatry in the process of planning and launching development projects should be accepted as greater than generally appraised by local leaders and national or international institutions.

The trend of contemporary psychiatry toward social treatment has renewed the confidence and expectations of psychiatrists in developing countries. El Guabal and other examples mentioned in this book attest to the efficiency of such efforts and urge others to follow them.

NOTES

1. U.N., *1965 World Social Situation*, p. 4.
2. Mead (Ed.), *op. cit.*, pp. 11–23.

INDEX

INDEX

Adams, R. N., 15
Adis, Castro G., 53, 59
Afro Americans, 19
  folk psychiatry, 63–65
Agriculture, 4, 25
  Argentina, 26–27
  Colombia, 73
  Uruguay, 27
  Venezuela, 24
Alcoholism, 38, 39, 41, 45–47, 74, 127
Alliance for Progress, 6
American Psychiatric Association, 53
Animism, 18
Arawak Indians, 62
Argentina, 4, 155
  agriculture, 26–27
  doctor/population ratio, 37
  population, 23
  psychiatric services, 42
  university enrollment, 36
Ayahuasca-Yaque-Caapi, 63

Barranquilla, Colombia, 78
Bastide, R., 65
Benalcazar, Sebastian, 77–78
Bogotá, Colombia, 75, 78
Bolívar, Simon, 72
Bolivia, 4, 37
  Indian population, 16
  psychiatric services, 42

Bouffee Delirante Aique, 64
Brazil, 4, 5, 24, 154
  candombe, 19, 63–64
  psychiatric services, 42
  slavery, 64
  university enrollment, 36
Brotman, R. E., 53
Buenaventura, Colombia, 29, 78
Buenos Aires, Argentina, 27, 42, 47
Bustamente, J. A., 64

Cali, Colombia, 59, 73, 77–78
  See also Pilot Plan of Social Psychiatry (PPSP)
Canada, 45
Candelaria, Colombia, 91–93, 99, 102, 144–47, 150–52
  prevalence of mental disorders in, 135–38
Candombe, 63–64
Carrizosa, A., 53
Cartagena-de-Indias, 19
Caudillos, 7–8
Centralism, 6–7
Chiape, M., 57, 60
Chibchas, 72
Chile, 46
  alcoholism, 45
  housing, 30, 74
Cities, migration to, 3, 11–12, 26–29, 51

Coca (*Erithroxicon Coca*), 61
Cocaine, 63
Colombia, 5, 59, 63, 154–55
  agriculture, 73
  death rate, 88
  development, 73–74
  geography, 72
  health resources, 74–76
  history, 72
  homicide rates, 45
  housing, 30
  illiteracy, 88
  "*La Violencia*," 74, 77
  population, 73, 87–88, 91, 167
  See also Pilot Plan of Social
    Psychiatry (PPSP)
Compadrazgo system, 13, 18
Conquistadores, 25
Costa Rica, 54
  alcoholism, 45
  housing, 30, 74
  psychiatric services, 42, 44, 53
Cuba
  santeria, 19, 63–64
  slavery, 64
Cults, 19, 63–65
Curanderos, see Witchdoctors
Curioso, 77

Dano, see Susto (fright)
Death rate, Colombia, 88
Deulofeau, V., 63
Doctors
  geographical distribution, 75
  /population ratio, 37, 74
  training, 100–102
Dominican Republic, 63
  suicide rates, 45

Ecuador
  Indian population, 16
  suicide rates, 45
Education, 34–36
Eisenberg, Leon, 50

El Cerrito, Colombia, 46, 138
El Guabal, Cali, Colombia, 46,
    87–91, 96–99, 144–47, 150–
    52
  data from registered patients,
    126–33
  medical students, training of,
    100–102
  neuroses, 138–39
  prevalence of mental disorders
    in, 133–35
El Salvador, 4, 45
Envidia, see Susto (fright)
Epidemiological research, 44–48,
    124–25, 164
Espanto, see Susto (fright)
Esquirol, Jean Étienne Dominique,
    42

Family life, problems of, 12–14
Folk psychiatry, 56–67
  Afro Americans, 63–65
  Hispanic American Indians, 57–
    61
  tribal Indians, 61–63
Fontanarossa, H., 47
Fundacion Hernando Carvajal, 89,
    119

Gran Colombia, Republic of, 72
Greenblat, Milton, 120
Guarani language, 17
Guatemala
  alcoholism, 45
  population, 17 23
Guyanas, the 19

Hacienda system, 30, 31
Haiti, 4, 5
  doctor/population ratio, 37
  voodoo, 19, 63–65
Hallucinogenic plants, 60–62
Hallucinogenic snuffing powders,
    62–6

Hispanic American Indians, folk psychiatry, 57–61
Holmstead, Bo, 62
Homicide rates, 45
Honduras
  alcoholism, 127
  population, 23
  psychiatric services, 42–43
  suicide rates, 47
Horowitz, A., 41
Horowitz, I. L., 35
Hospital Psiquiatrica San Isidro (HPSI), 79, 80, 117
Hospital Universitario de Valle, 79
Housing, 29, 52
  Chile, 30, 74
  Colombia, 73–74
  Costa Rica, 30, 74
Hudgens, R. W., 47
Huenlin, D., 4, 28

ICT, *see* Territorial Credit Institute (ICT)
Illiteracy, 52, 74, 88
Indians
  Arawak, 62
  Hispanic American, 57–61
  institutions, 17–18
  Mojo, 63
  traditions, 16–17
  tribal, 18–19, 61–63
  Tucano, 62
Industry, 4, 7, 25, 51–52, 73
Inquisition, 19, 63, 72
Institute of Nutrition for Central America and Panama (INCAP), 38
International Committee Against Mental Illness, 119

Jamaica, 19
Jani, see Susto (fright)
Japan, 22

Jaspers, K., 122, 123
Jones, K., 157
Juvenile delinquency, 39

Kallawayas, 60–61
Kiev, A., 56, 57, 59, 65, 163

"*La Violencia,*" 74, 77
Lambert, J., 154, 155, 157
Latifundia, 26
Lehman, D., 25
Leon, C. A., 45, 46, 57, 59, 74, 134, 136, 137, 156
Lewis, Oscar, 53
Life expectancies, increases in, 36–37
Lima, Peru, 29, 46, 47
Lindgren, J. E., 62
Lipset, S. M., 10, 22
Lower classes, 11–12
  psychiatry and, 52–54
Luis H. Garces Center, 86

Machismo, 127
Mal de ojo (evil eye), 57, 59
Maleficio, see Susto (fright)
Malnutrition, 38, 51, 52
Marari, 63
Marginality, 30–31
Mariategui, J., 46
Maternal deprivation syndrome, 50–51
Mead, Margaret, 84
Medellin, Colombia, 73, 78
Media, 12, 27
Medical students training, 100–102
Mexican Americans, 16
Mexican Indian Institute, 16
Mexico, 4, 19, 154
  homicide rates, 45
  Maya civilization, 17
  population, 15, 17, 23

Mexico (*cont.*)
  psychiatric services, 41, 42
  public health services, 37
Mexico City, Mexico, 27
Middle classes, 11
Migration to cities, 3, 11–12, 26–29, 51
Mojo Indians, 63
Munoz-Bautista, C., 47

Nahuatl language, 57
Narcotic addiction, 38, 61
Narvaez, Calderon, 41
National Institute of Land Reform (INCORA), 73
National Plan of Mental Health, 155
New Granada, *see* Colombia
Nurses, 74–75
  training, 102–8

Obeah, 63, 65
Oetting, E. R., 54

Pan American Health Organization, 42, 43
Panama, 4
  psychiatric services, 42
Paraguay, 44
  Indian population, 17
  psychiatry and lower classes, 53
  public health services, 37
Pasmo, see Susto (fright)
Pasto, Colombia, 80
Paternalism, 7, 8, 30, 31, 119
Perdomo, R., 105
Peru, 54
  homicide rates, 45
  Indian population, 16
  mal de ojo, 59
  psychiatric services, 42
  public health services, 37
Peyote, 61
Pilot Plan of Social Psychiatry (PPSP), 44

assessment, 143–47
educational activities, 94–112, 145–46
  allied personnel training, 102–8
  doctors and students training, 100–102
  psychiatrists training, 95–99
  public education, 109–12
facilities, description of, 86–87
  Candelaria, 91–93
  El Guabal, 87–91
in future, 161–67
  education, 162–63
  expansion, 161
  organization, 166–67
  research, 164–65
  therapy and prevention of illness, 165–66
launching, 79
objectives, clarification of, 83–86
optional models, 154–60
  alternative approaches, 156–58
  local action, 155–56
  as national plan, 154–55
  prerequisites, 158–59
organizational activities, 113–21, 146
  leadership functions, 118–21
  teamwork functions, 114–18
practicability, 148–52
research, 122–39
  data from registered patients, 126–33
  epidemiological, 124–25, 164
  field surveys, 133–39
Pinel, Philippe, 42
'Plan Piloto de Psiquiatria Social,' *see* Pilot Plan of Social Psychiatry (PPSP)
Planned parenthood, 38, 87
Political traditions, 6–8
Pollution of water, 37, 38

Population, 3, 26–27, 50–51
  Argentina, 23
  Bolivia, 16
  Colombia, 73, 87–88, 91, 167
  Ecuador, 16
  Guatemala, 17, 23
  Honduras, 23
  Mexico, 15, 17, 23
  Uruguay, 23
Populism, 8
Portugal, 26
Possession, 64–65
Poverty, 3, 30–31
Prostitution, 38, 39
Psychiatric epidemiology, 44–48
Psychiatrists, training of, 95–99
Psychotropic drugs, 60–61
Puerto Rico, 63

Quechua language, 57
Querido, Ari, 85, 105, 113

Rappee, 63
Reid, D. D., 137
Research, 122–39
  data from registered patients,
    126–33
  epidemiological, 124–25, 164
  field surveys, 133–39
  need for, 122–24
Ribeiro, R., 19
Rio de Janeiro, Brazil, 27, 29
Rockefeller Report, 24
Roman Catholic Church, 7, 19,
    57–58, 64, 72
Rube, A. J., 57

St. Louis, Missouri, 47
Salas, Peru, 60
San Juan Bautista Parochial Cen-
    ter, 89–91
San pedro, 60
Sanitation facilities, 37, 38
Santeria, 63–64

Santiago de Chile, 44–45
Sao Paulo, Brazil, 27
Schultes, R. E., 60
Seguin, C. A., 58, 59
Seitz, G. J., 62
Shanty towns, 29
Slavery, 19, 63–64
Snuffing, 62–63
Social classes, 9–12, 52–54
Social programs, organization and
    planning
  education, 34–36
  public health, 36–37
  social diseases, 38–39
  social security, 33–34
Social security, 33–34
Spain, 6, 25–26, 72
Stainbrook, E., 64
Stein, W. W., 54
Suicide rates, 45, 47
Susto (fright), 57–58, 65

Tegucigalpa, Honduras, 47
Territorial Credit Institute (ICT),
    74, 78, 87, 89–91
Trance, 64–65
Trapp, 35
Tribal indians, 18–19
  folk psychiatry, 61–63
Trinidad, 19
Tucano Indians, 62
Tzutzil language, 57

Unemployment, 27
United States
  Alliance for Progress, 6
  suicide rate, 47
Universidad del Valle, Facultad de
    Medicina de, 78–81, 119,
    155, 163
Urbanization, 25–27, 51–52
Uruguay, 154–55
  agriculture, 27
  population, 23
  psychiatric services, 42

Veliz, Claudio, 6
Venereal disease, 38
Venezuela, 5, 63, 154
    agriculture, 24
    suicide, 45
Vilca, 61
Villanueva, 86

Voodoo, 62–65

Waikas, 62
Water pollution, 37, 38
Witchdoctors, 18, 59, 60, 98
Women, position of, 13, 19
World Health Organization, 42, 84